RAILWAY SEASON

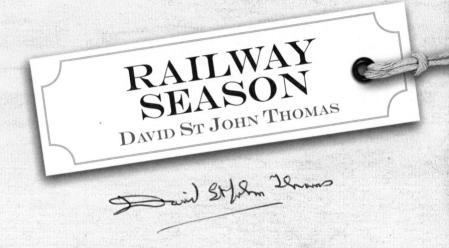

RAILWAY
SEASON

DAVID ST JOHN THOMAS

F

FRANCES LINCOLN LIMITED
PUBLISHERS

First published 2011

Frances Lincoln Limited
4 Torriano Mews
Torriano Avenue
London NW5 2RZ
www.franceslincoln.com

RAILWAY SEASON

British Library Cataloguing in Publication data
A catalogue record of this book is available from the
British Library.

ISBN: 978-0-7112-3259-4

Printed and bound in China

10 9 8 7 6 5 4 3 2 1

CONTENTS

Summer

Autumn

INTRODUCTION

ESPECIALLY IN THE days before serious road competition for goods, the railways were driven by the seasons. The volumes of traffic and their nature changed week by week. At roughly the same times of year, though with changing emphasis, the focus was on a succession of different places large and small. This greatly added to the colour.

When my Australian daughter-in-law suggested I write a similar volume to *Fishing Season*, published by Exisle, my son's Australian and New Zealand publishing house, I immediately saw the possibilities. Always hating the 'not-invented-here' culture, I also loved the format and welcomed the challenge of being author of that rarity, a railway book dependent on words rather than pictures.

However, since trains never travelled between continents, the interest is largely insular, especially perhaps for those of us in Britain where railway history is longest and most complex. While happily Exisle are taking an edition of this work to fit into their series, it had to be originated in the UK. While exiles support a 'down under' fascination in Britain's railways, there is little reciprocal interest.

The country railway in the British Isles has always been a special interest. While this book is about the whole of our railways, by their very nature most lines run through the countryside. That London was able to grow so much in the 19th century was mainly because milk and fresh produce could be rushed in from further away and there was no need to retain land for livestock and their fodder. Rail-served suburban development enabled London and other big cities to stretch their tentacles into the deep countryside, yet even in inner-city areas commuters are all too aware of 'leaves in the line' or 'wrong kind of snow'. Nature keeps us on our toes.

The Industrial Revolution was under way before the arrival of the first passenger-carrying public railways as we know them, but its fruition depended on trains to carry raw materials and finished goods. Cheap and speedy post, instant news via the railway adjunct, the electric telegraph, the standardisation of time and the creation of national brands were all railway induced... distances effectively shrinking as lines through the countryside carried faster and more frequent services. In the days when half the value of companies traded on the Stock Exchange was represented by railways, the weekly receipts which were the key to the nation's prosperity depended on variations season by season and year by year.

Much of this has been taken too much for granted. For example, as a boy in the West Country I noticed that the *Torbay Express* had seven coaches in winter instead of a minimum of eight in summer, and heard that steam heating worked the locomotive's boiler as much as hauling an extra coach, but never related it to the continual seasonal changes on the rails. Yes, people returned home for Christmas, and fog could be a hazard, yet the general full ramifications of the seasonal throb still were not appreciated. I hope I bring them to life in the following series of short chapters. They have certainly been fun to write, bringing together things I've known for up to half a century combined with fresh research.

WINTER

SOUTH MOLTON AGAIN

ESPECIALLY IN THE days before serious road competition for goods, the railways were driven by the seasons. Nowhere was this clearer than at South Molton, where as an evacuee I saw several annual cycles. It was as an unofficial signalman at a hard-pressed crossing station on the lengthy Great Western Barnstaple branch that my love and knowledge of railways developed.

The guard's van, with its young trees and plants wrapped in straw, day-old chicks and calves, was as seasonal as the extra early spring goods trains bringing in fertilisers, and the autumn rabbit special, while horse and cattle fairs created intense activity and, even in the war, summer Saturdays required extra passenger trains. Everyone took an intense interest in the crops of the fields through which they passed, and conversations between train and platform staff were largely about which farmers were doing well and those who needed to pull up their socks.

In the grim days, when most nights German bombers flew unchallenged overhead to bring mayhem to Midland and northern towns, the seasons somehow kept people normal and seemed almost more important than departing servicemen (some never to return) and soldiers coming home on brief leave. With the parallel road carrying little more than American tanks, even for local journeys people came back to the trains, though seldom was there need for anyone to stand (and then only until the first few stations out of Taunton) on the customary three-coach ones.

The staff realised that the line was living on borrowed time – though its busiest days were actually those immediately after the war, when some summer Saturday expresses carried destination boards: 'Wolverhampton, Birmingham and Ilfracombe'. Rapid decline followed till the last trains (now passenger-only though traditionally goods had been far more important) ceased in 1966.

My *Country Railway*, whose chapter on South Molton proved the most popular, followed ten years later. Though it was nostalgic, that was well over forty years ago, and at least a generation since the BBC asked me to do the last of several pieces from the old platform. Though curiously the North Devon Link Road, which crosses a widened viaduct west of South Molton has reopened vistas once only seen by train, what was a totally different way of life has disappeared into history, remembered only by the oldest of us.

When recently I passed by the station which had been my childhood haunt, access was barred, though an earlier occupier had proved friendly and lent me papers he had found, including parcel receipts which showed how the railway had brought in the town's first fresh fish as it had national newspapers, mail-order shopping, and Burton-on-Trent beer.

And there was the pub, the Tinto, to which passengers retreated when trains were late. It suffered when they ran more punctually and carried fewer people. It closed well before the railway, an event I recorded on radio, almost singing Auld Lang Syne solo, since, in encouraging others to get started on its final Saturday night, I forgot the microphone in one of my waving hands.

What memories of riding on the Mogul or once, in a swap with a passenger train, a Bulldog as it performed the daily two-hour shunt in the goods yard, and of occasional footplate trips to the next station, the driver once reading one of my father's poems aloud en route. It was always the human activity I most enjoyed. Some characters might have stepped out of a late Victorian novel. Many were illiterate, ignorant of luxuries taken for granted by townies, and took little interest in the war, food rationing hardly touching them. Though the railway was the link to the outside, few locals had gone beyond Taunton. As in much of rural Britain, the long-distance journey to 'join-up' was the first by many recruits.

When my Australian daughter-in-law suggested I write a similar volume to *Fishing Season*, published by Exisle, my son's Australian and New Zealand publishing house, I immediately saw the attraction. Always hating the 'not-invented-here' culture, I also loved the format and welcomed the challenge of writing that rarity, a railway book dependent on word pictures rather than photographs.

However, since trains did not travel between continents, the interest is largely insular, especially perhaps for those of us in Britain where railway history is longest and most complex. While happily Exisle are taking an edition of this work to fit into their series, it had to be originated in the UK. Exiles support a 'down under' fascination in Britain's railways, but there is less reciprocal interest – though I've always enjoyed their railways.

While this book is about Britain's railways as a whole, by their very nature most lines run through the countryside. And that London was able to grow so much in the 19th century was mainly because milk and fresh produce could be rushed in from further away and there was no need to retain land for livestock and their fodder. Rail-created suburban development enabled London and other big cities to stretch their tentacles deeper into the countryside, yet even in inner-city areas commuters are all too aware of 'leaves on the line' or 'the wrong kind of snow'. Nature keeps us on our toes.

The Industrial Revolution was under way before the arrival of the first passenger-carrying public railways as we know them, but its fruition depended on trains to carry raw materials and finished goods. Cheap and speedy post, instant news via that railway adjunct, the electric telegraph, the standardisation of time and the creation of national brands were all railway induced... distances effectively shrinking as lines through the countryside carried faster and more frequent services. In the days when half the value of companies trading on the Stock Exchange was represented by railways, the weekly receipts which were the key to the nation's prosperity depended on variations season by season and year by year.

Thank you South Molton station and its staff not merely for giving me purpose in the war but for setting me off on the quest that has led to numerous books and sharing memories and understanding with so many people.

It also brought surprises. I had dim memories of an official-looking gent coming into the signalbox one black-out evening. He asked: 'Is it all right if I wait here. Where's the signalman?'

'The train's half an hour late. He's down at the Tinto and you have time for a quick one.' He shook his head. 'Or you could stay here. The notice on the door [now on my wine cellar door] says visitors aren't allowed but you could sit there.'

He then asked questions of a kind nobody else ever did. Unusually interested, I thought. Nine or ten years later I was asked to visit the District Superintendent at Exeter. 'You owe me a favour', he announced. 'Remember I caught you signalling a train at South Molton. I should have turned you out but you seemed to know the rulebook better than the signalman would, so I let you be. But now you can help me.' Which naturally also helped me in my new role as journalist.

SNOW

THE CONDUCTOR WAS magnificent. Ten times the normal number of passengers had boarded the Aberdeen train at Elgin. 'Now folks,' he said. 'Because of the snow, we'll not be at our best today, but before those of you who would have gone by road start making hasty judgements, remember we're at least running. Sorry about the crowds. Anyone using a seat for luggage, please remove it before I come through. Seats are for sitting.' He them came into the lightly-patronised first class section, asking if he could bring in others without seats, but would we like first to change our seats. When he brought the others in he told them: 'These gentlemen have paid expensively for peace and quiet. Please respect that.'

Though with such crowds, station stops were inevitably longer and we had to slow at one point where the train brushed branches of trees bent down by the weight of wet snow, we were only a few minutes late into Aberdeen.

It was a typical example of how all but extreme snows benefit the railway. Years ago before they closed, it was as though on snowy days the clock had been put back at many country stations. People who had long gone to work by road walked to the train and waited for it to arrive round the waiting room fire – perhaps late, possibly delayed by mainline connections, but definitely running. Dr Beeching's cuts were sometimes greeted with the pained: 'What'll happen when it snows and the roads are dangerous?' In many areas the train is still seen only as an insurance policy should it snow.

Unrealistically, many people have always felt that the railway should be there for odds and ends of traffic when needed... such as late on Saturday night when traditionally trains ran later than buses. Then BR felt an obligation to do everything possible, however expensively, to keep trains moving right up to the time of closure of a route. Thus the original line over the steep Dava to Inverness via Grantown-on-Spey and Forres was reopened after a severe snowstorm only days before all traffic ceased.

So we have our first mention of snow causing serious trouble in the Highlands. There is a long history of problems, though, until the severe winter of 2009-2010, snow ploughs stationed at Inverness had for decades been sent to help out in England far more often than they were used locally. Nothing more forcibly tells of how winters have generally become milder than the miles of decaying snow fences that used to protect the track from drifting. No repairs have been made in recent times, while the precaution of trains carrying emergency rations on the Far North Line has seemed anachronistic.

The winter of 2010 was notable not merely for low temperatures but the length of the freeze-up. Inverness was for a time cut off from the south with blockages on both the mainline to Perth and the Aberdeen route. On the last day of March, a Glasgow-Inverness service became stranded in a drift near the highest railway point in Britain at Slochd Summit, on the 'new' direct route from Aviemore to Inverness.

A following ScotRail train disgorged its passengers at Aviemore to stay in hotels while it went to the rescue. However, it became stuck short of the first train, whose 107 passengers were not rescued until 1.30 next morning. A third train with snowplough, food, water and blankets had tried to reach the stricken one, but itself became stuck 300 yards short, resulting in laborious digging of a path and carrying the relief supplies.

The West Highland line also experienced a prolonged closure, with several avalanches on a windswept section between Upper Tyndrum and Tulloch. Because conditions were unstable, for a while engineers clearing the drifts had to be withdrawn. Eventually 15,000 cubic yards of snow were removed. Fort William trains were diverted to Oban, and passengers taken on by bus.

Especially in the Highlands where the railway is often in a more exposed position, the balance has changed, roads generally being kept open more reliably if expensively because their use is much greater. That however doesn't apply to high passes, notably Drumochter, where motorists frequently find the snow gates closed, or to occasional extreme blizzards. It is because that part of the A9 was closed early one morning that passengers off the sleeper that temporarily terminated in Perth found there was no connecting bus. Reopening the mainline was complicated by a spectacular derailment of an Eddie Stobart Tesco train closing the passing loop at Carrbridge just before another snowstorm.

At the beginning of that 2009-10 winter, on 22 December, the brand new LNER Peppercorn A1 Pacific headed *The Cathedrals Express* from Victoria to Dover and back, being one of few trains to move in Kent that day. On the return trip, to the delight of enthusiasts relishing old technology winning over new, it rescued about a hundred commuters, dropping them at their home stations.

Before motoring days, replacement bus services didn't exist, and frequently passengers were stranded… and at the least likely times of year and places. As everyone who has studied GWR history knows, two Great Blizzards hit different parts of the system in 1881 (six passenger trains snowed up between Reading and Oxford) and, in 1891, in the West Country in the last year of the broad gauge.

Though many fewer people travelled then, one shudders to think of what happened to the passengers of the 1st and 2nd class only express nicknamed *Zulu* on Monday 9 March. It took from 3.00pm that day until midday Friday to reach Plymouth having been snowed up most of the time at Brent. Also on that Monday, the earlier *Dutchman* was derailed at Camborne.

After an early spring, the sudden cold snap caught everyone unaware, the whole of the South West being seriously dislocated in a way that was still much talked about in my youth, as was indeed the gauge conversion of May the following year when the passing of the last-ever much-loved fast broad gauge expresses with their 8ft single-driver locomotives caused much emotion. Amazingly the conversion of virtually the whole system west of Exeter caused less disruption than had the Great Blizzard – though there was no road alternative for passengers over the long weekend when 4,200 men drafted in from every part of the GWR achieved a carefully-planned miracle.

The trouble with snow is that even with today's sophisticated weather forecasts it is hard to predict exactly what quantity will fall exactly where or be driven into drifts by how strong a wind from exactly which direction – nor, as became a national joke when fine powdery snow penetrated engine works, whether it will be 'the wrong kind of snow'.

The cruel winter of early 1947 was better remembered for shortages, of heat, coal, three-hour electricity cuts and general misery. Timetables were curtailed and some branches totally closed just as things had begun recovering after the war. Older readers might remember that, due to gales preventing colliers sailing south in the North Sea, the railways stretched every muscle to maximise the use of coal trucks. Many goods stations were kept open over the weekends, the nine o'clock radio news daily featuring the number of wagons emptied around the country.

There were also heavy snowfalls. A friend who was a new conscript recently moved to Parkhall Camp served by a halt on a military branch line near Oswestry, recalls how 200 men crowded into two non-corridor suburban coaches with six-aside seating hauled by a saddle tank engine. They proceeded downhill along the Cambrian mainline toward Welshpool when they stopped just short of a drift.

There were shouts of 'everybody out'. Jumping down, we found railway officials handing out enormous coal shovels. One of our four groups began to dig at once into the cutting in front of the train, while the other three set off along the cutting sides. The fourth group carried on to the end of the cutting and began digging back. Thus we tackled the clearance at four places and seem to complete it remarkably quickly. Hearing the beat of steam exhausting from cylinders, we flung ourselves into the snow as the little train came clanking through, checking we had dug the drift out wide enough.

With us once more aboard, the little tank engine proceeded to push us back towards Oswestry. The snow had yet to relinquish its hold. Coming to what seemed a particularly stiff climb, the train slowed to a halt, the little tank manfully chuffing away at the rear, wheels spinning. Too slippery by half. Steam was shut off and, as the driver ran off the incline. We found ourselves going back into Wales. Then he put her back into reverse and with regulator fully open charged the slope.

He did a bit better this time, getting further before once again we slowed to a halt, wheels spinning and the engine chuffing away. Problem. But the driver had no intention of spending the rest of the day on this incline. Again we reversed back, but this time much further – seemingly to where the gradient reversed. The driver then opened up everything and, with the two carriages bouncing and swaying drunkenly from side to side, charged the slope, the speed diminishing all too rapidly. But we just managed to reach the crest.

That left little time to prepare our gear for inspection upon which depended leave for the weekend. Yes, we did pass, but only just. Rather than given credit, we were warned that, when we returned from that longed-for weekend, we should find life even harder as the instructors fought to bring us up to their standards. But not for me. I had no idea as I hurried to the train south that what I thought was a minor injury to my hand incurred during the 'dig' had been infected. Rather than return to Oswestry, I would find myself in Chester Military Hospital.

Such scenes were not uncommon in the 1940s and 1950s when heavy snowfalls hit different parts of the country. One of the effects of the West Country's worst blizzard of the 20th century is mentioned in the final chapter. It began on Boxing Day 1962. I was snowed in for a week on the edge of Dartmoor, keeping in touch by telephone for a daily report on the railways' battle to get back to normal for *The Western Morning News*. This included an account of how the final trains on the Great Western's Launceston branch were unable to run. Indeed for a couple of days very little ran in the West Country. The Southern's route round the north of Dartmoor had just been closed. Reopened when the Great Western's to Plymouth was blocked, the first goods train sent that way became stranded. With no mobile phones, Control had to wait for the enginemen to phone in from a remote farmhouse which they struggled to reach.

It has never needed much snow to disrupt the Southern's third-rail electrified system. Best remembered are the reports of how freezing, frustrated passengers risked their lives by jumping down and walking along the track.

Virtually nowhere in Britain is immune to snow, but until recent times the most frequent falls and drifts were in northern Scotland. Until its closure, the Buchan system north east of Aberdeen especially suffered. Much of the route along the gently undulating land exposed to gales from many directions was a particular sufferer. Valiant were the efforts of staff, especially signalmen, to reach their posts hoping to keep the traffic moving, fish being vital.

Throughout the country, blizzards brought special discomfort to the signalmen who began working in two different boxes as conditions started to improve. With 10-hour rather than 12-hour shifts not only did it take them up to two hours to walk between boxes for their four-hour stint in each, but they had to reach one at the beginning of their day and return from the other. That practice has long been abandoned, with eight-hour duties in boxes open continuously – and statutory rest days. It was the relief signalmen who then faced the greatest struggle if snow prevented driving. The more recent centralisation of signalling brings its own problems – and we still suffer from frozen points since only key ones on mainlines are heated.

In all walks of life people were once prepared to make greater sacrifices to get to their posts than today when disruption is seen as more normal. The prolonged closure of lines after an accident becomes a 'crime scene', and scheduled 'blockages' to relay track, must make them feel less needed when faced with illness or snow. However, throughout railway history passengers have praised railwaymen for their dedication in snow storms, washouts, accidents.

Nowhere were staff more loyal than on the Highland Railway with its mainline serving thinly-populated country with few employment opportunities all the way from Stanley Junction, just north of Perth, to Wick and Thurso. And nowhere did staff have to struggle with such adversity. Crossing trains at lengthy passing loops with points having to be changed locally at both ends called for brisk attention in good weather, and in snowstorms was unpleasant if not worse. In the Highland winters of yesteryear, the fight against the elements was continuous

Steadily the Highland Railway spent lavishly by its local standards to protect the line with snow fences, a V-shape sloping pair of them on either side of specially vulnerable cuttings to prevent snow falling on the track. Signal wires were sited high, above the likely snow line. But there were blockages a plenty, and not a few derailments, including a spectacular one of a goods train hauled by a pair of Jones 4-4-0s north of Killiecrankie station when it ran into a snow drift in which a large tree, blown down by the wind, was buried.

No two blizzards were quite the same and consequences varied sharply. Staff sometimes suffered long periods of icy isolation and hunger and, before food for emergencies was carried, passengers could become weak with cold and hunger. Yet there were lucky ones, notably two crews whose trains were stuck at a passing loop near a pub where they enjoyed the life of Riley on continuous overtime for several days. In the past, there were often few passengers on the northern section of the Far North Line beyond Helmsdale, where it turns inland and crosses a largely uninhabited moor.

Rather than cite a catalogue of snow incidents, let us conclude with more detail about a single episode which highlights the difficulties when there were numerous signalboxes but no mobile telephones. It is based on a pair of articles by Richard Arden in the magazine of the Friends of the Far North Line, a lively group including Richard which has inspired great improvements to the train service and its usage in recent years. They are based on records kept by Syd Atkinson, operating manager at the time of the troubled week beginning on Friday 27 January 1978.

It began snowing furiously on **Friday 27 January 1978. On Saturday 28 January:**

11.45 Forsinard reports points blocked by snow and no communication with Helmsdale.

Afternoon: other blocks fail around the Highlands.

18.55 Inverness-Euston stalls on the route over Slochd Summit, is drawn back to Culloden Moor and sent via Inverness and Aberdeen. Slochd route ploughed. Two down trains long delayed at Aviemore now able to proceed, the 9.40 from Euston (having made a special stop to pick up stranded motorists) arriving at Inverness at 03.43 next morning.

22.09 The 17.15 Inverness-Wick leaves Forsinard. 23.09 Georgemas says it hasn't arrived. Wick engine to Georgemas ready to assist.

Sunday 29 January:

00.50 Engine heads cautiously toward Forsinard, headlights on and whistling.

07.30 Police asked to help Tomatin signalman. Unable to do so. Neighbours eventually supply food after he's been in the box 18 hours.

07.50 Wick engine back at Georgemas having become stuck in drift but dug out about a mile short of Altnabreac. After crew change at Wick, the engine takes PW inspector to try and get through to Forsinard to find last night's 17.15

09.35 Georgemas signalman hears from driver of 17.15: five coaches derailed, two engines and one coach with 70 passengers gone forwards about 1½ miles, stuck in drift. Two miles of track damaged behind derailed coaches.

11.05 Wick rescue engine re-enters section, but a pair of wheels derailed and stuck on drift approx 1½ miles short of stranded locos and coach. The general manager and Thurso police alerted.

14.25 Dingwall reports 08.45 special from Kyle of Lochalsh which departed Garve at 11.20 hasn't arrived. Loco and PW staff rescued at 16.05.

16.10 Carrbridge reports Inverness plough derailed poking up about a foot in the air. Meanwhile all wires and telephone poles down from the Mound to Golspie. Wick without phone communication, so station assistant reports from Thurso: three helicopters on way to Saturday's 17.15.

17.13 All passengers safely landed at Halkirk or at Wick airfield, PW and some other staff airlifted at 21.00 when further block failures occur on Far North Line and on mainline between Blair Atholl and Inverness.

11.38 Perth to Aviemore halted at Blair Atholl, passengers given refreshments in hotel and returned to Perth. Haymarket at Aberdeen ploughs operating from Blair Atholl and Inverness respectively.

Monday 30 January:

07.44 Dingwall loco and PW staff head north to clear line of poles and wires. Get stuck in snowdrift near Kinbrace.

16.07 Inverness tool van heads north, leaving Helmsdale 23.10. BBC News reports that three bodies found in cars under 20ft of snow on A9 near Ord of Caithness.

Tuesday 21 January:

06.00 Snowing heavily again. Inverness plough rerailed at Carrbridge but coach of empty train behind it found derailed. Aberdeen plough stuck, derailed one mile south of Altnabreac. Engines return to Forsinard for wire rope to pull it clear, achieved by 21.00

Wednesday 1 February:

Carrbridge to Tomatin cleared and some trains now running but only with ploughs of which there is a shortage and clearance through drifts minimal. Aberdeen plough again stuck in same drift as yesterday but released by 21.00. Helicopters take Army personnel from Fort George to clear Caithness blockage.

Thursday 2 February:

Aberdeen plough stuck again, not reaching damaged track till Friday. Rerailing delayed until Sunday.

Friday 3 and Saturday 4 February:

Haymarket plough again needed to keep Perth line near Drumochter clear.

Sunday 5 February:

The line now clear of obstruction and track relaid beyond Helmsdale.

05.24 Inverness PW workers' train leaves Inverness for Forsinard.

06.56 Inverness combined plough and crane depart for Forsinard.

17.00 Two coaches rerailed.

Monday 6 February:

04.00 Locomotive and four coaches pushed back from Forsinard to Helmsdale.

05.00 Plough back into Georgemas-Forsinard section.

16.15 Two engines and final coach follow it back out. Plough returns to rerail final engine and track repaired by 17.05. So after nine-day blockage ironically the first train is again the 17.15 Inverness-Wick which passes trouble spots at walking speed.

One can only guess the cost in today's terms and wonder how things would work out in a similar storm now with radio-signalling and no staff between Dingwall and the two northern termini.

A DAY IN THE LIFE OF
A COUNTRY TERMINUS

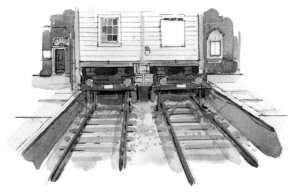

OUR IMAGINARY STATION is a cross between several real country termini and typifies things in the greater West Country (including what Devon and Cornwall people might regard as distant England) in the 1950s. Long closed and mainly demolished, a few relics still attract a trickle of enthusiasts. The stationmaster's house with fifteen yards of platform is now a stylish home.

A scraggy patch of rhubarb shows where there used to be an allotment. The branch line whose terminus it was, was recently the subject of another book, and enthusiasts also occasionally consult its timetable in copies of *Bradshaw* and early BR ones.

In Diesel days when the freight was concentrated at larger stations, the branch ended as a straight piece of track with no pointwork in a buffer at the end of a single platform. If you were to tell the staff of the early 1950s that this was to happen, they wouldn't believe you, so permanent, unchanging had things been.

After all, the line snaking down the cutting into the station had for generations been the gateway not just to the little town but the whole region. It had brought everything innovative: instant communication on the telegraph, national newspapers and the first of the nationally – branded goods, technology – and above all ideas. The famous and infamous had walked across the platform, together with tourists, youngsters going off to London to work and returning for holidays, and soldiers treated as heroes returning from wars, the loved ones of those who didn't return always remembering their earlier emotional farewell there.

The railway was part of the fabric of life and death and, though there had been increasing competition, it remained so at the beginning of the 1950s. It was still unthinkable that its day would end, firstly with severe economy, and – after a bitter row – finally one, bitter, January Saturday night.

So let us go back to the 1950s. Now there are still two platforms, one with a run-round and the other a bay. Both can take a seven coach train, the maximum allowed on the branch. Other than for stabling purposes, the bay platform is normally used once a day. The goods reception line, where the daily goods is broken up and re-formed, is next to the run-round and, beyond, there are three sidings where trucks can be unloaded and a coal merchant has his depot. The goods shed is at the extremity. Six wagons can be loaded and unloaded under cover.

The engine shed is on the other side, next to the bay platform and is approached by a single track with coaling and watering facilities. Because our branch line has its junction at a rural location, not at a major station, it retains its own engine and shed. Many others have lost theirs, it being cheaper to run a light engine morning and evening.

The signalbox is at the platform's end, overlooking the station's throat, and convenient for the engine men to use as their base between trains. Except when trains cross at the terminus, when the signalman collects the single-line token, the driver normally takes it to the signalbox. One way and another, there is surprising activity. Someone not familiar with railway practice might question whether it's all necessary or there isn't an element of playing trains.

On weekdays there are seven passenger trains (an eighth on Saturdays) plus the daily goods. Apart very occasionally for engineering work, on the Sabbath the branch line sleeps, and locals feel free to walk along it, especially enjoying spring-time flowers. Though occasional lorries load and unload goods, even on weekdays, the terminus sleeps between periods of activity.

Yet thirteen people, all men, are employed by the railway here. That includes pairs of engine men, guards and signalmen for early and late shift. Among the others, there's a lamp man who cleans the lenses and tops up the oil on the signals here and at the one other station with signals, the intermediate crossing station. There is a booking clerk and a parcels porter on a staggered single shift including covering the others' duties for a couple of hours at the beginning and end of the day, a goods clerk and two railway lorry drivers. All are supervised by the stationmaster who works gentleman's hours but makes unexpected visits at other times. He alone lives on the spot in the old-fashioned station house which goes with the job.

The weekly wage bill greatly exceeds the takings. Especially in summer, many more visitors arrive than locals leave and, though there is an occasional rush of fish from the nearby seaside town and of soft fruit sent as passenger parcels, little goods traffic is originated. However, the one intermediate station with a passing loop and signalbox, also under the stationmaster's jurisdiction, has a quarry whose traffic yields real income and occasionally requires a second goods train.

The staff are a collection of responsible, strong individuals who somehow cohere into an efficient and usually friendly team. Days off sick are scarcely known, but duties are sometimes swapped and shift times changed to suit needs.

Though he is respected, which the autocratic relief who usually takes over is definitely not, the stationmaster is the least intellectual of all members at the small town's Rotary Club meetings. Several other members of staff hold their own better in the outside world. The parcel porter is a leading member of the local meeting of the Society of Friends, and one of the engine drivers a keen member of the Methodist Church choir. He often sings a hymn to his mate, though we can only guess at how appreciated that might be. Gently spoken and always cheerful, they would fit in anywhere.

The signalmen wouldn't. One lives and breathes his pigeons. The parcel porter always invites him to release carrier pigeons which occasionally arrive in a wicker crate for training flights home. The other signalman, tall and gaunt, is hot on swear words, sandwiched into factual messages: 'The 9.17 is – running eight – minutes late, –it.' But he cares about his job, and waves at each driver arriving or setting off.

The signalbox is spotlessly clean, the lever handles brightly polished and a cloth always held to pull them. Engine drivers and other visitors, the stationmaster on his daily visit not excepted, are expected to wipe their shoes.

Not that the rest of the station is unwelcoming. The fire lit early by the young, tall lamp man is a positive joy. The signalmen and he both 'borrow' coal from the locomotive when the formal allocation runs out. The platforms are swept daily and snow promptly brushed off their edges.

Even the goods porter in his lean-to against the goods shed keeps his space spotless, but he's the most aloof member of the team, a keen reader of mysterious books kept out of sight. Though the pigeon-loving signalman periodically dives into a tome on his subject, the *Daily Herald* is as far as the pleasure reading of others stretches. A single copy does the rounds, starting and ending in the signalbox, where the stationmaster scans it. But there are the circular letters detailing train alterations and special workings with which many have to familiarise themselves. Though they don't have great aspirations, none of the staff are illiterate. Indeed, as are their own children in the railway tradition, they were expected to do better than most at school.

So while they remain blissfully ignorant of the troubled times that will soon affect them all, let us see them about their daily tasks. Currently the thing most still dread is the day they will retire and get under the feet of their wives. They mainly live in small homes and, though they 'aren't doing too badly', haven't had money or tradition to develop hobbies. After retirement, they'll pop back to the station, at least weekly for their pension, and occasionally to take advantage of the free or cheap tickets to which they are entitled. Maybe several will also continue to tend lineside allotments cheaply rented from 'the company'.

First person on duty in the early morning is the fireman who lights the fire on the branch prairie (2-6-2) tank engine, swapped with another each Saturday for maintenance. Next to turn up is the engine driver, followed by the signalman, whose first duty is to signal the engine out of the shed road and back onto the waiting two-coach non-corridor train. This is done earlier in winter, to provide steam heating for passengers' comfort, than when the weather is warmer.

The booking clerk arrives after the first passengers and spends ten minutes or so issuing tickets, often at least one to London, before going home for his breakfast, resuming duty when the day's first down train arrives just over two hours later.

The routine that follows, which will be repeated with few variations roughly each two hours, is then set in motion. Typically, the signalman signals the engine around the train and into the engine shed road, where the fire is raked and the boiler's thirst assuaged. The porter loads a barrow or so with parcels and enters them in the ledger in the parcels office. The booking office clerk collects, cancels and sorts the tickets before opening his hatch to serve the handful of passengers already waiting for the train's next trip. A bus from the nearby seaside town comes into the station yard, adding half a dozen to those buying tickets and leaves with a similar number. The bus used to be railway owned and, perhaps unusually these days, still comes to the station, calling at the small bus station on its way. A couple of taxis take away arriving passengers, and one comes to drop a departing one. The next car however is from an outlying farm; the couple of boxes of trays of early strawberries grown under glass are on their way to Covent Garden. As yet there's no competition from Continental growers and the high price – even in 1950s money sometimes £1 a pound – justifies the carriage and packaging. One or two farmers still have to 'make their mark' as they cannot sign their name when despatching or receiving parcels (including day-old chicks and the occasional young bullock).

The stationmaster, his uniform topped with hat, meets day-time trains and sees them off, chatting with locals. However, on the day's fourth train he leaves for the branch's only other station served by a signalbox for his daily visit there. Today is going to be a busy day there, for spring is a busy time for road building and the traffic from the quarry means a second goods train will be needed to take away a string of loaded trucks.

There is just time for him to glance at the one daily goods on its way to our terminus, which crosses (passes) the passenger in the loop. Tokens are exchanged. The second goods, only to the intermediate station, will follow once the passenger has reached the junction. And then it is the time when the extra Saturday passenger train – the only normal one through from the nearest large town – comes down the branch bringing home some workers still on a five-and-a-half day week. On its return trip, it takes a miscellany of locals going shopping, to a football match or cinema, or just to meet a friend.

Meanwhile at our terminus the goods train will still be doing its daily shunt – yes, still even on Saturdays. It takes the best part of two hours, with another visiting engine. Back and forth it goes picking up and pro-pelling trucks into the sidings, perhaps putting a truck in place for side off-loading a tractor or other farm equipment, just where horse-drawn carriages and early motors once were. Steadily the departing goods is put together on the loop.

Early in this ritual the signalmen change shift, which they do earlier on a Saturday to give each a long weekend: early turn one week, late the next, year in, year out, apart from a fortnight's holiday when a relief signalman arrives by car.

After the raking of the fire and taking on water, the goods is ready to go, but backs into the bay platform (if it is at maximum length its tail placed separately in a siding) and waits till the arrival of the next passenger train. The local engine crews now change duty, the late duty ones chat with those of the goods train in a somewhat crowded signalbox. It being Saturday, the weekly change of engines between the local shed and the larger one in the market town also now takes place. As the early duty ones slip away for their long weekend, the rest of the staff have a few minutes of intense activity as the engines are swapped, the signalmen furiously pulling levers until both trains have their new engine in place.

First, the arriving passenger train engine runs round and visits the engine shed. Then what has been the goods engine backs onto the passenger train. The engine now taking the goods re-makes up the train in the loop line and is soon ready to leave. It will come back on duty as the branch engine the following week.

The passenger will not follow for another half hour. According to the traffic, it might or might not overtake the goods at the intermediate crossing station. That is one of the few decisions the staff on the spot normally take themselves.

There is only one pair of non-stop passengers on the branch, a July and August Saturday-only mid-morning special, made up of four to six through coaches to London, attached to an express at the junction, and its opposite number from London in early evening. At present the historic practice of sending down empty stock in time for the up service and the down train returning empty is still followed. But there's a hint that to save money the through coaches might travel from London and back in the day, giving return visitors a somewhat late arrival back in the capital. False economy say our staff. The stationmaster is furious. 'It could just about work till the down express is so late that the return service cannot leave on time. Then it will be improvised chaos,' he says, adding: 'Put everybody's nose out.'

There's already been one less controversial change. Though the last but one daily train is well used, except on Saturdays when it was known as the fish-and-chippie, the last of all used not to be. True, it brought a handful of passengers from London, especially on Fridays. Few of them had heavy luggage and a bus now provides the connecting service from the market town, though increasingly people drive to meet their loved ones off the express. There is however a strong case (and one that will probably be agreed) for its restoration on Saturdays when the bus is often full and standing.

The change allows the branch and its signalboxes to close nearly two hours earlier, but the loss of the last up train for which there is no bus replacement means that parcels including flowers and strawberries have to be delivered early. The stationmaster isn't anxious to point this out, because an unwelcome alternative could be the branch losing its engine, the trains being stabled at the market town. It would kill the very spirit of the branch.

Shorter hours means less overtime, but with recent wage improvements that's OK by the staff, who also want to enjoy a better lifestyle. They shudder at what their fathers and grandfathers seemed to accept without argument. Throughout Britain each section of the railway is very protective of itself.

And 'Why not?' one might ask. The railways thrived on local pride. We know what happened when that was taken away. So let us leave our country terminus while continuity is far more evident than change. The timetable varies little between years, and the unusual – blockage by snow, derailment, strikes, Sunday School specials and once even a visit by the *City of Bristol* taking visitors to a different place for the fortnight straddling August Bank Holiday: they're soon forgotten as almost holy regularity resumes and many people without watches tell the time from the passage of the trains.

WATCHING TRAINS

Since the opening of the first wooden plateways, watching trains has been a very British obsession. While travelling around the world, I've noticed that though Britons may not be the keenest of observers of passing scenery, more people walking or working near the railway turn their heads to take at least a cursory glance at what is passing here than elsewhere. Perhaps we still celebrate that railways were our gift to the world.

The trains themselves have become much less interesting, with the loss of so many of the features of yesterday: locomotive trains with a variable number of passenger coaches according to the season, many displaying destination boards, often to multiple places. Once there was a fascinating range of restaurant and kitchen cars, and larger, untinted windows were easier to look into so one could see how profitable the patronage was. Not merely are today's trains nearly all of standard lengths, but they travel faster, and it's harder to tell where they are going – though across the country the range of destinations is much reduced. Another point, while their liveries are more varied than in the Grouping Era, their roof lines are more uniform. The GWR especially had trains composed of many different types of carriage – though most appreciated the horizontal division of the chocolate and cream coaches, enhancing the impression of length. Few of today's carriages have that, and continuity is spoilt by doors picked out differently.

In steam days the biggest attraction naturally was the locomotive itself. On the same trains, on different days, it could be of a different class. Anyway it was individual, proudly displaying its unique name. Named trains once also sported their own particular headboard. When steam specials run on mainlines, they now attract exceptional crowds, enjoying the sounds, smoke and steam, and peering into the footplate. Travelling on the footplate, as on one of today's many preserved railways (see Railways for Pleasure), one feels like Royalty with people waving and taking photographs round every bend.

Though the locomotives were usually unnamed, those hauling goods trains were by no means without interest. They were working harder, and there was usually more time to study them and exchange waves with the crew. The goods trucks themselves were fascinating, in pre-nationalisation days including wagons of different companies and styles, and many private-owners, sales of whose miniature versions for model railways still flourish. Most of today's goods trains are block ones composed entirely of the same kind of wagon carrying the same load. They move more quickly, and lack the guard's vans of yesteryear which, again of differing designs, one always noticed, including in winter smoke from the stove pouring out of the chimney.

Banking engines have also largely disappeared. The Lickey, south west of Birmingham, was one of many inclines where train spotters especially congregated. They would hear the whistle codes between banker and train engine as they prepared to start, and judged how the work was apportioned between them as they slowly puffed, pulling and pushing their way up the hill. In the opposite direction, on goods trains, before vehicles were fitted with continuous brakes controlled by the driver, engines had to pull against the force of the hand brakes, manually applied truck by truck before the train began its descent.

Some watched mailbags being exchanged at speed and water scooped up from the troughs between the rails and, on many single lines, tokens exchanged at speed between lineside apparatus and an arm stretched out from the footplate. Such physical contact between train and land have ceased – along with slip coaches and other curiosities.

Added to that, nearly all signalling is now remotely controlled, and semaphores (of varying regional patterns) have largely been replaced by automatic electric light signals. They tell if the sections ahead are clear, but not if a train is soon to pass. Even the neat rows of telegraph poles, and their variable number of wires once a prominent feature, have disappeared. Standardisation, standardisation.

Yet still many people feel compelled to wait for a train to pass. The number taking photographs is greater than ever: railway photography has become a major industry in its own right. There's keen competition to see work reproduced in one of the railway periodicals whose photographic standards are always reaching new heights. That is despite the fact that on some stations, there's been a running battle between photographers and petty bureaucrats who in some cases have insisted on erasing shots and even retaining cameras, supposedly in the interests of security. Though the major operating companies spell out their perfectly acceptable codes, some narrow-minded staff still insist they know better.

Even high-ranking officials can be offensively officious. Until not so long ago one could be televised on almost any station without need for permission or 'facility fee'. But I was speaking to the camera at the buffer stop at Windermere, when a trio of stout officials waddled from the train and stood in front of the camera to stop proceedings. Could we show them we had paid the facility fee? Yes, we could but the money was wasted because the sequence was spoilt, and the schedule didn't allow us to wait for the next train. Is it any wonder that railways sometimes receive a bad press?

Watching trains has many guises. Scenic routes, especially where the railways run through gorges or alongside the sea, are naturally popular points. The railway press gives advice on the best locations. The band of younger enthusiasts who still avidly collect engine names and numbers, now congregate around depots where frequent sightings are likely. Traditionally they used to be at platform ends, paying an old penny for a platform ticket. After the unsuccessful experiment with open stations, the new automatic barriers, which only accept valid travel tickets, has made it harder for those not travelling to reach the platform; to see people off or welcome them, and help them with their luggage, or just to look around or use the station's range of facilities. Once I enjoyed going down to the furthest end of the platform, serving the 'throat', where platform tracks link with each other and reduce in number, as at Charing Cross, where the platforms reach the river bridge or at Euston or King's Cross for the classic departures of trains north. Even if one has a travel ticket, today someone quickly asks what you are doing.

When I was nine, I started collecting GWR engines and numbers, aided by the company's locomotive book for 'Boys of All Ages' listing them all with good photographs, diagrams and potted histories of the different classes. Rapidly, however, I discovered there was much more to train and station watching. My pennies for platform tickets brought great joy. Especially in the days when there were fewer long-distance but much heavier and longer trains, each arrival and departure, with branch and stopping service connections, was an occasion.

There was an air of expectancy in the days before electronic displays as a porter picked out the appropriate board with a pointing hand at its end and positioned it in the stand. Another porter pushed the gas container to replenish the restaurant car's supply. Even when passengers started to congregate, using the then plentiful seating, there was still time to look at connecting stopping trains and see how many (or usually few) passengers transferred to the awaited express. Most were usually country people, a few possibly bringing produce to market. Each stopping train's guard's van was emptied, often with produce, some destined for the express. Just a glance told you what the season was and eavesdropping on conversations told of good or bad ones.

The sense of occasion was enhanced by the fact that in those days services included many one-offs, at Leicester the *Waverley* for Edinburgh and the *Thames-Clyde Express* for Glasgow. The same is true in Germany today, the timetable skilfully comprising trains with very different starting and terminating points. Joining trains with through coaches for different points necessitated making sure one chose the right coach, something especially important on the 'portmanteau' Atlantic Coast Express mainly consisting of single all-purpose coaches for each resort.

At important intermediate stations, by the time the approach signal dropped, porters would be assisting many passengers, possibly checking their seat reservations. A crowd lined up near the platform edge before the train could be heard and then seen. At most stations, trains came in swiftly, stopping at exactly the right spot. There was much to be done.

The restaurant car's gas supply would be increased, a red flag fixed to it to prevent movement. A barrow might bring supplementary food and, if anything was short, one of the stewards would dash to seek a replacement at the depot or refreshment room. Usually a comparable number alighted and joined, the arrivals asking for directions, especially to connecting services. A cascade of luggage, suitably rearranged in transit in the guard's van, was transferred to waiting barrows, whose place was quickly taken by those with luggage to load. Unless it had recently replenished its tanks from a trough, the locomotive might take on water, or occasionally the engine changed. If coaches were being added or detached, they would be handled by the station's pilot engine, a porter jumping down onto the track to connect or disconnect. The wheel tapper went his way making a reassuring ringing sound.

I enjoyed every aspect of it, but nothing more than seeing all the human activity, the eventual centrepiece being the station inspector, intensely checking his watch and seeing what doors remained to be closed. Miraculously, the gas supply was cut off and the red flag removed, the engine ceased taking on water, its driver was eagerly looking out, the stoker building a good fire, the huge luggage doors closed and everything else happened almost at once. Everyone knew the allotted time, the last porters who had helped sort out passengers in their compartments perhaps cutting it finest. The station inspector pushed the plunger to tell the signalbox all was ready. As the platform clock's minute hand moved, the train was on its way.

I felt I had discovered much about how the railway operated and served its customers, and the part of the country we were in. It beat collecting engine numbers, though I usually finished standing by the locomotive looking at it in awe and then could see the whole train pass as it gathered speed, the guard often giving a final wave, for in those days railway staff got a kick out of being in the limelight and encouraged the interest of younger people. The public were not a nuisance – or danger. Some teachers said it would be easier without the pupils or perhaps the parents, but never did we hear that kind of sentiment from railwaymen.

In the middle of the day, up and down services often arrived at intermediate stations within a few minutes of each other (porters just having time to change platforms), sharing the same connecting services. Then there would be a long gap, Today's pattern of more frequent, shorter, standardised trains suits the marketing department. In the age of the car, a long gap between trains endangers people driving themselves. So there would be time to go to one of the refreshment rooms or, on major stations if one was not broke, for an excellent three course lunch, pudding laid in one's absence if explaining the 'need' to see another train, possibly a non-stop, meanwhile. No question of not being trusted; luggage could be left with impunity.

What a lot we have lost, yet how much still survives: hundreds of tons of metal thundering along the 4ft 8½ins-gauge on its narrow strip of land through the countryside, with gentle curves and gradients. Trains may be noisy when passing, but how much better that is than the constant drone from a busy road. Stations, too, still appeal… when access is possible.

However, though the passenger may be spoilt for choice of train, the luxuries of yesterday have far from progressed into being the necessities of today. At termini, trains can no longer be joined a leisurely twenty minutes before departure, or a meal ticket collected from the chief steward on the platform. And no longer do passengers entering a third or standard-class compartment gasp 'Oh it's first class' as they did in the early days of British Railways when generous three-aside seating in compartments beautifully finished in varied named timber greatly uplifted standards. Recently on the North Yorkshire Moors Railway, I went into a well-kept compartment of that era and made the mistake of offering the guard a first-class supplement, payable on the train. 'You should know: there aren't anti macassars', he teased. Each era has its good and bad points but, while all is not by any means lost, for me and many other discerning people with long memories, the best days are well past. And so many changes and cut backs have happened in recent years that the railway industry can by no means boast high morale.

Summer Saturdays (see separate chapter) were another tale, with many more and crowded trains, poorer timekeeping and generally lower standards – but a fantastic offering for train watchers out in the country or by the coast or at big stations which became as populated as mini-cities. Many branch lines then had through trains or coaches: an operator's nightmare and a schoolboy's dream.

Especially if facing a crisis, such as being in hospital, waiting to go to the operating theatre, it can be rewarding to run through one's personal memories. Most people's will begin in childhood. Mine start watching Continental expresses, and through trains of goods wagons that actually went on the ferries, pass through Gidea Park, where we lived and had our first model railway, very much GWR in LNER territory.

Older readers might recall the Hornby 0-gauge 'Model' of *Caerphilly Castle*, a crude 4-4-0 version of a 4-6-0, which Hornby couldn't have got away with for several generations since. What magic, in a taxi when I was just seven, the very first Great Western engine I saw was *Caerphilly Castle*, charging past as though we were standing still on the parallel road. As the family layout developed in Devon, the most favoured engine was *King George V*, produced by Basset Lowke.

Another moment of magic, still just before the war, was being invited on the footplate of the real thing for a ride down the length of Newton Abbot platform just after it had returned with the bell presented on its recent American tour, where its power proved equal to that of much larger local machines.

Meanwhile we had spent a year at Harpenden. Absenting myself from the local public school during games, I found 'The Hole', a secret place beside the track just north of Harpenden Junction, where the extraordinarily little-used Hemel Hempstead branch left the express lines but, more importantly, stopping passenger trains were switched from the fast to the slow lines. North of here, the slow lines were solely for goods. Lengthy trains mainly of coal, a few hauled by Garret-articulated engines, crawled under permissive working to wait for their turn to continue further south when the passenger traffic allowed. Expresses were short, feather-weight affairs still in the Midland tradition whose red had become standard on the LMS.

Though the GWR had my main affection, Paddington being the most classy terminus serving the most classy system, visits to London were not complete without refreshment at the café on the old bridge across Liverpool Street, watching and hearing suburban trains: the gush of air as the tank engine bringing them in was released, rapidly to follow the return working with its new engine. But what filth, and general absence of style except perhaps for passengers already being served their pre-dinner drinks on the night Continental boat express. I dreamt of what it would be like waking up at the Hook of Holland; it was to be many years before I first travelled abroad but steadily built my repertoire of British memories.

Glasgow with its four termini (and sooty lower level platforms at two of them) was another wondrous place. Point rods seemed permanently on the move at the Central's throat out over the Clyde. In train movements it was Britain's busiest station, as Liverpool Street was in the number of passengers handled. There was a wonderful long teak unit in which boards displaying details of individual trains were as the Scots say timously inserted by a couple of busy attendants. It survived so long and was such a talking point that there were hopes it might be retained as a functional period piece. Not to be — any more than the unique 'company bike' for Nairn's signalmen to hasten between the boxes at either end of what is Scotland's longest platform. Ridicule about it being long overdue for modernisation killed that oddity and caused expenditure that could have been better used on other things

In Edinburgh, the steep gardens overlooking the quadrupled track heading north out of Waverley popping in and out of short tunnels before reaching Haymarket, provided a bird's eye view of great and varied activity, while at Inverness, evenings witnessed non-stop activity in the days of steam with several nightly sleeper trains and Motorail services. In the time-honoured way, trains from the north backed into the station next to those to the south with which they were connecting, and those from the south backed into the north-bound platforms also to provide cross-platform transfers.

The Sea Wall between Teignmouth and Dawlish is where I've seen most trains pass or, on summer Saturdays, be halted by adverse signals, those controlled by Old Quay, Teignmouth and Parson & Clerk signal-boxes all coming into play. But watching trains in less familiar places, notably at junctions (Kemble for two branch lines), Ross-on-Wye, Moat Lane Junction, Dovey Junction and others between single-line routes, has always had a particular appeal. Branch line junctions were especially subject to long periods of idleness punctuated by frantic activity, with engines taking on water and greater emphasis on parcel business than we have become used to on surviving lines.

Sometimes the setting was as important as the train, as at Cadleigh in the Exe Valley. Or the interest might be engine against gradient, enjoying the sight and even more the sound of a dirty, worn-out loco struggling up the Long Drag, the Settle & Carlisle, miraculously saved from closure with less interesting trains but now thoroughly modernised and playing a major passenger and goods role.

The list could go on. Nearly all England's northern cities had great stations, many several. Not so southern England where electric trains came and went with as little fuss as buses or trams. But while I loved the GWR's Snow Hill, happily reopened, I was never comfortable at Birmingham's two-in-one New Street and even less passenger-friendly as rebuilt.

Wherever there are trains, people will consult their watches or show off their knowledge, if only to themselves. As said earlier, train watching is very much alive in the country that invented them.

THE INALIENABLE CHARACTERISTICS OF THE COUNTRY RAILWAY

COUNTRY RAILWAYS CAME in many lengths and forms but shared certain inalienable characteristics. Being constructed more cheaply than mainlines, they hugged riverbanks or contours more closely, meaning sharper curves and steeper gradients. Bridges were used sparingly, level crossings common, especially in the flatter half of Britain. Many stations were situated beyond a comfortable walk from the towns and villages whose names they bore, for the cost of reaching the centre wasn't justified.

Yet the stations were generously if not prodigally built, including decorative features. Especially after the coming of motor competition, they looked ridiculous for the meagre traffic many handled. Signalling was also wasteful because greater growth was assumed than actually happened. Thus there were separate up and down platforms even where one would have sufficed.

The pace of life was not just slower but of a totally different order from that on the mainline. Natural rural conservatism, and a wish to be polite to customers, steep gradients and the need frequently to replenish the locomotive's small water tanks, all slowed things down. Services were usually sparse, perhaps only four or five a day, seldom more than eight or nine. Some lines still open actually have a better service now than when trains had a monopoly.

Spoilt by having some of the world's best mainlines, the English poked nostalgic fun at the quaintness of the branch line, yet in most cases it should have been more rustic. For example, virtually all platforms were built high so that passengers could step straight out of their carriages. At some places a moveable box positioned to help those who couldn't use a step would have saved much. Economically speaking, a lot of lines shouldn't have been built at all, and many others only on a rudimentary basis, lower costs raising the break-even threshold.

The trouble was that both the investing public, and the Board of Trade who controlled safety, tended to regard a railway as a railway, making inadequate distinction between trunk route and rural feeders. Certainly many promoters were unable to keep their horizons realistically modest. So even the branch line connecting a single town with the junction was often seen as forming the first part of an eventual through route, and the station may have been inconveniently sited in readiness for the extension that was never built. Lines that were actually started as part of trunk schemes spent their days serving purely local needs. The four weekdays-only all-station trains on the hilly Aberystwyth to Carmarthen run were using the only completed section of the Manchester & Milford Railway. When you look at your local line, assess not only what was built but why, and what expectations were fulfilled and unfulfilled.

Many lines were developed as part of a warring strategy of attack and defence as the major companies tried to extend and consolidate their territories. The only laudable result from wasteful duplication was that trains came to serve a further string of villages and hamlets. Often these hoped-for inter-city routes were given bridges for double track, though usually only one was ever laid.

Country railways were built with persistent optimism, the traffic potential of a single valley being grossly overstated in the prospectus, and capital raised through all kinds of local business and human motives rather than from careful proof that the project would be self-supporting. Sometimes local farmers and landowners cajoled the nearest mainline company to put their valley on the map, or threatened it by seeking help from the nearest rival company, however illogical a link to that system might have seemed. Elsewhere, especially in western Britain, the local people put together their own scheme using their own money and buying-in expertise. Shares were almost invariably later sold to the nearest big company for half or less their original price.

It doesn't follow that the landowners, farmers and mill owners, who lost a large part of their money, in fact struck a bad bargain. Almost always the opening of a railway led to an immediate drop (often by almost half) in the price of the then staple coal, needed even for ploughing, and crops were significantly more valuable at the railhead than even a dozen miles away. Milk could be worth half as much again if sent fresh by churn to a city than if turned into cheese or butter for want of quick, cheap transport.

The railway being the universal carrier of everybody and every-thing going any distance, its opening brought new hope to valleys and towns which had so far been unserved, losing out to rival places. In the final analysis, perhaps few lines failed to make their mark even if running at a loss. But this would still have happened if they had been less expensively equipped and operated.

That rural railways could be built more cheaply is a point often made by the experts of the time. The need for greater flexibility was reflected in a little-used Act of 1864 allowing Light Railways, built to a lower standard, the axle load to be limited to eight tons and speed to 25mph, and built with the consent of landowners without resort to Parliament. More practical was the 1896 Light Railway Act estab-lishing the Light Railway Commissioners who could grant Orders without involving Parliament. But old attitudes died hard and many of the Light Railways were built in unnecessarily complicated style with elaborate stations never justified.

Britain was criss-crossed with railways and few villages were ten miles from a station, yet we lacked the truly rural lines that flourished on shoestring budgets in some continental countries, notably France. The Irish story is similar to the British, though yet more pathetic. Again there were two separate pieces of legislation, failing to bring real changes in attitudes. Some of the Irish 'standard narrow-gauge' 3ft lines might have seemed quaint but still involved waste and unneces-sary ritual which came with the railway always being a railway.

In Britain and Ireland, the fate of the country railway became pro-gressively more unhappy. In Britain, railways first met bus competition by investing in buses themselves and using them as feeder services. But then the 1930 Transport Act created a controlled monopoly, allowing railways to profit as major shareholders in bus companies but stopping them running their own routes. So they could neither compete, or properly integrate services. Passenger traffic quickly dropped on most branch lines, especially at stations a long way from the places they served, but goods of all kinds still largely came by train and still only minor savings were made.

It was the steady disappearance of goods traffic after nationalisation that led to astronomical losses. Savings, such as simplifying signalling and withdrawing staff from lesser-used stations, still went against the grain and, if made at all, were done so grudgingly. Though Diesel cars were successfully introduced on the narrow-gauge County Donegal in Ireland and on the GWR well before World War Two, and had the obvious advantages of starting up at short notice, not requiring a fireman, and avoiding an engine having to run round its train – steam power was still pretty universally used. Again though the GWR had introduced many unstaffed halts as extra stopping points for its push-pull auto trains in the 1920s and 1930s, as did the Western Region after nationalisation, other regions – notably the London, Midland – resolutely resisted such commonsense. Unbelievably, it insisted that staff must meet every train or the station be totally closed.

Unstaffed halts and pay trains did not spread nationally until well after Dr Richard Beeching's savage cuts of the 1960s. Some key lines that closed then could still be active today had their operation been simplified. Over the years millions could have been saved. Officials and policies were in a time warp. Thus a thousand steam engines were built after nationalisation, and new staff who would later be expensively made redundant continued to be recruited. At many stations two men, plus holiday and sick reliefs, were pointlessly employed in a signalbox rarely did more than one train pass at a time. Little-used goods stations were kept open even when close to busier ones. In the 1950s nobody seemed interested in making the most obvious of savings, leading to the necessary but over-severe pruning of the Beeching cuts. Such had become the losses that there was neither money nor time for sensible reorganisation.

So watching the excessive staff congregate on the platform under the eye of the stationmaster remained one of the time-warped joys of the country railway. Over the ages there have been many photographs of country stations with staff proudly lined up in their uniforms. Looking at them, I often wonder what they all did. Remember that pre-1914 they would each be working at least a ten-hour day, a 5½-day week, and have no paid holiday. With such hours and such pride in their work, it is no wonder that stations were spotlessly maintained, their gardens among the brightest in the land.

Yet the branch line with no staff, no human-controlled points and signals, that just end at the buffer stop – the glorified siding normally worked only by multiple-unit trains – is both useful and attractive. The 'basic railway' is at its best where the station buildings have been taken over privately or where they have been demolished and replaced by a bus-type shelter.

All stations, open or closed, buildings new or crumbling, have their interest. In the early hours of the morning the fireman would book on to light up the valley's only locomotive in the days when the railway was a little self-contained, privately-owned affair. Now the shed may be a farmer's store. The signalman was often left to work out his days in splendid isolation; at best, one can usually only trace the foundation of his box. The goods yard will have its own tale: the coal merchant may still store coal here, or did so until recently. Abandoned buildings may include a mill that closed soon after the coming of the railway in the 1850s because it could not meet the competition of bigger mills at the nearest larger town. The arrival of trains was not a blessing to all.

How much of a closed line remains depends on development pressure. In south east England whole complexes quickly disappear under housing estates but, half a century after the last train steamed out in furthest Scotland, some stations remain virtually intact except for the rails. In his Scottish volume in the 'Forgotten Railways' series, John Thomas vividly describes the railway that once ran through half the length of the Great Glen and was among the first to close in Britain: 'Straddling as it does country of great splendour it is a wonderful line to walk. The piers rising from the Spean and the Oich speak of a glorious aim that was never achieved. The Invergarry & Fort Augustus Railway, carved out of the mountain slopes, will be there until the rocks melt with the sun.' And, it might be added, as a monument to over optimism, playing politics and wasteful practices.

On most country lines still open, the railway interest is now secondary to the scenery, that totally different view of the world, winding among the Welsh hills or running along the top of a Lincolnshire dyke, a few intimately following the coast, sometimes on and sometimes under the cliffs, as on a long stretch of the former Cambrian Railways route from Dovey Junction to Pwllheli.

For sheer seaside splendour in colour, you cannot beat the short St Erth to St Ives branch in Cornwall winding along the cliffs over pure white beaches and often a Mediterranean-blue sea. Typical of such branches, today it ends in a simple buffer stop. The huge area once occupied by a longer platform, run-round, shorter bay platform, sidings and goods yard is now a popular car park, though ironically the increased number of trains brings many from the park-and-ride at the new station of Lelant Saltings.

All the great Scottish scenic lines remain open too, but only because, belatedly, costs have been pared to the minimum, helped by radio signalling. No longer do strings of signalboxes have to be manned for the passage of a single train.

Wherever you go in stopping train Britain, note how prodigious were buildings and other facilities when capital and labour were cheap and how it took railwaymen far longer than the public they served to adjust to changing times. What losses and hardship could have been prevented had realism struck earlier.

SPRING

A COUNTRY JOURNEY
LIKE NO OTHER

PERHAPS THE BEST way fully to experience the seasons is to travel repeatedly on a route through the countryside. Many readers, especially longer-distance commuters, will surely have their own memories, but scarcely anyone can have travelled so regularly over many years on a more delightful route than I did from Newton Abbot to Paddington, leaving and returning at all times of the day, sometimes making the return trip the same day.

I first used the route before the war and quite often in the late 1940s and 1950s. When I became especially familiar with it in the 1960s, the Great Western influence was still strong. Newton Abbot station, like Paddington, had been rebuilt between the wars specially for the holiday traffic, and there were greater variations in the train service and number of passengers between the seasons and days of the week than now.

Another difference: people got started later in the morning. The first arrival in Paddington used to be at 12.15pm, just in time for a lunch appointment. Such was then the perception of the West Country's remoteness, that many of the people I lunched with were amazed I'd just 'come up'. Though with longer non-stop runs and certainly less congestion, some steam trains were as fast as today's High Speed ones, though in the 1960s the day's first express still took four full hours.

As business travel increased, that became less than two and a half hours with a 10.00am arrival, after a splendid non-stop run from Taunton to Paddington. It has deteriorated somewhat under privatisation and, whereas every train had a full restaurant car, at the time of writing, the *Golden Hind*, though no longer so called, is one of only two trains on the entire former Great Western system now to boast one. Virtually all my journeys included breakfast, lunch, afternoon tea or dinner. On day trips breakfast and dinner.

It was often straight into the welcoming restaurant car, the splendid scenery beginning almost immediately: a glimpse of Dartmoor over the racecourse, down the Teign estuary, along the Sea Wall between Teignmouth and Dawlish, up the Exe estuary, a spurt of speed over Exminster marshes and a great view of Exeter Cathedral. You could tell the time of year from the number of waders in the estuaries at low tide. In winter departure could be in darkness. Occasionally the sun was caught rising out of the sea. The state of the sea told one much: a storm brewing up, or a vigorous swell following one while, in the teeth of rough weather, at high tide great foam from breaking waves actually doused the train.

All the way, there were a hundred and one seasonal indicators. In spring, swans were often seen nesting near Exminster, where the sidings (all lifted years ago) were used to store wagons not in seasonal service, for example for the West Cornwall early broccoli business, or the transport of cattle, long a thing of the past. The length of trains of returning milk empties showed how productive cows were, more Cornwall and Devon milk going to London in winter than in late spring when supplies were greater from nearer to the capital and much in the West Country was turned into butter or cheese.

But I'm getting ahead of myself. Brunel's daring route on a ledge under the sandstone cliffs between Teignmouth and Dawlish came at a price. There have been many breaches in the wall, and cliff falls have always been a problem (there is now extensive netting), especially when frost penetrates them after high rainfall. The profusion or otherwise of the mesembryanthemums (see end of chapter on the Natural History of the Railway) tells one how harsh a winter it has been. The amount of water pouring down Dawlish Water through the gardens indicates what recent rainfall has been like. If I'm alert there's just time to glimpse the black swans and in spring and summer, maybe a cygnet. In summer, the number of visitors on the beaches including Dawlish Warren says how good a holiday season it is. I've switched to the present tense since I still make occasional journeys, remembering just where to look.

Out of Exeter, the freshwater Exe keeps the train company and then into a gentler land with many familiar landmarks such as a distinguished house, church and the paper mill at Hele which I recall specialised in making something called SEB, a coarse sheet filled with air which wonderfully bulked out cheap books.

The M5 hugs the railway as it sweeps round a prominence and from both, the velvety turf of Cullompton Bowling Green can now be seen. Pointing it out was a family ritual. The Culm is now near us, and the motorway rises over a bridge over the route of the Culm Valley branch to Hemyock, though its last traffic (milk) ceased well before its opening: extra expense in vain. We're now into rich red arable country, whose crops have changed greatly. There are now patches of yellow rape, occasionally of gentle blue flax, and one field of blackcurrants, all harvests dependent on the season.

Beyond Tiverton Parkway the Grand Western Canal comes into view. This Tiverton arm was all that was built of an ambitious scheme to save mariners' lives by a broad cut from the Severn to the Exe estuary. The reeds speak of the season, with an occasional glimpse of water lilies in summer. Into Whitehall Tunnel marking the division between Devon and Somerset, with a view of the monument to the famous Duke of Wellington who foresaw the social change the railway would make and hated it, dashing through what used to be Wellington station and faster still down the rest of Wellington Bank where man was first reputed to have travelled at 100mph.

Then, noting where the Barnstaple and Minehead branches came in at Norton Fitzwarren, into Taunton, with a glimpse of the private school, kids' dress reflecting the season. In the old days, no one coming into one's compartment at Taunton meant having it to oneself all the way to Paddington. When not in the restaurant car I preferred the less popular very front.

And now what specially gives this route its character. In so-called crowded Southern England, the largest place we race through between

Taunton and Reading is modest Newbury. It really is a rural route. For the first two miles to the junction with the Bristol line, we are between the Bridgwater & Taunton Canal and the River Tone, and then we join one of the Great Western's 'cut offs' to shorten the journey. Opened in 1906, it brought Devon and Cornwall just over twenty miles closer to London. It was mainly built by labourers earning six old pennies an hour, reduced with loud complaints to 5¾d.

They must have caused as much disruption in this neglected area as the original navvies in the mid-19th century. It is now over half a century since I first wrote that the express trains racing across the willow-growing flat lands, still flooded in winter when I first came this way, had as much relevance to local life as aeroplanes flying overhead. The water table is still high, and willows are still grown for basket work, but no longer are places cut off when flooded but not deeply enough for boats to be used. Past the Isle of Athelney, where King Alfred is supposed to have burnt the cakes, standing proud of the surrounding flat land. Until Langport, accompanied by the flood-prone River Parrett, we're actually on the GW's Taunton-Yeovil branch, the rest of it long closed. This part had to be substantially rebuilt, changed out of recognition, for expresses.

We're soon into Somerton Tunnel where, unless you take preventative measures, the pressure hurts the ears, and then through the village that was once the county town but where the mean local autocar service came far too late to make much difference to economic and social life. The next section with a viaduct across a delicate valley has always been a favourite, and then through places gently reflecting their names that could only be Somerset: Charlton Mackrell and Keinton Mandeville. At Castle Cary we join what had been the long Weymouth branch from the GWR's original Bristol route near Chippenham.

I never come this way without noting the connection Parliament insisted should be built with the Somerset & Dorset whose route we soon intersect. While built, it was never used. Cussedness in railway politics is nothing new.

In a series of curves, we have vaguely followed the winding River Brue up to Bruton, a lovely little place. There might be a lengthy stone train waiting to follow us at Witham, and then a fast ride near to the River Frome until the start of the Frome cut-off, shortly followed by the Westbury one. In one of those futile theoretic cost-cutting exercises, closure of both was mooted but soon forgotten.

Just beyond Westbury are two landmarks: Westbury cement works whose tall cooling chimney can be spotted for nearly twenty miles, and one of the famous White Horses, simply formed by the removal of turf from the chalk soil. It has always been a fast stretch through the Vale of Lavington. Next I look out for the approach of the remains of the Devizes branch at what used to be Patney & Chirton station, where once the push-pull auto-car, on which I made a round trip lasting several hours, leisurely reversed with only a couple of passengers.

Then we are into another of the journey's delights, the Kennet & Avon country. The canal had long been closed and neglected, lock gates collapsing, and it has been great watching its steady restoration and increasing business. It disappears into a tunnel on one side and emerges on the other at Savernake just beyond which is the tall restored Crofton pumping house, built to ensure there's enough water at this high level. Also to note are the remains of the parallel lines (the fruit of more strife between companies) from Marlborough and the expensive extension to the east to enable trains of the once lively but impoverished Midland & South Western Junction to pass without having them punishingly delayed by the GWR.

Between times I'll have noticed the crops, seen a pheasant or kestrel, occasionally a red fox warily keeping close to a hedge but unafraid of the train. Over the years also the dire effects of Dutch elm disease. Though there's still nice mixed wooded country, it is mainly eyes on the canal with waterside pubs and other features to Hungerford. There I first see us crossing the genteel High Street and then where a derailed stone train knocked down the signalbox with the signalman still in it. Concentrating on the long-distance holiday traffic, the Great Western served such places badly, and it is good that now the franchise named after its august predecessor has semi-fasts as well as stopping trains.

Still with the canal usually beside us, at high speed we pass through Newbury, once served by three branch lines, and then Newbury Racecourse station, very much a seasonal affair. Still the canal is with us: a living thing, home to ducks, moorhens and swans, occasionally spoiled by too many boats moored up. Spring ducklings and cygnets are a special joy.

Though this is obviously now commuter land, it remains largely unspoilt, productive countryside even around Aldermaston, until ever-expanding Reading's first estates came into sight. It was around here that one hoped for, and usually enjoyed, an uninterrupted non-stop run through Reading. Not merely do nearly all the trains now call there, but in both directions one is usually delayed before being signalled into a platform. Extra trains may be very welcome, but the result has become heavy congestion. At the time of writing, work is about to start on an ambitious rebuilding, giving more platforms. It may not be completed during my travelling days, with the promise or threat of electrification possibly adding further years of disruption.

From Reading to Paddington the run used to be exhilarating, the Castle or King and later Diesel engines and then the High Speed Train showing off their paces but, especially where the Heathrow Express comes in, today there are usually delays. Seldom is it an uninterrupted ride into Paddington, often with further delay on the final approach. And that is before Crossrail brings new traffic across London. The GWR may have only run a sparing service of trains of up to fifteen coaches, yet many were faster and more reliable, all once having a string of branch line connections. The huge increase in shorter ones has once again come at a price. Even then Crossrail is to terminate at Maidenhead rather than logically reaching Reading.

However enjoyable it was talking in the club-like restaurant car, those of us going to London for business enjoyed silence for the final part of the journey. Once when loud Americans were making themselves a nuisance, to the horror of other passengers, I joined in, then adeptly silencing them by saying that perhaps we should follow the time-honoured practice of keeping quiet for the final half hour. Winks all round.

As we run through station after station, overtaking slower trains, run alongside and then cross the Thames, and pass art deco factory, gasometer and other minor landmarks in an increasingly built-up environment (gone are Sutton Seeds' trial grounds and most other open spaces), I'm reminded of my thoughts on journeys of years ago when I planned something exciting or prepared for a crisis meeting. A lifetime of broadcasting, book writing and publishing memories are unlocked.

Though porters have gone, and tickets (once collected on board) have to be inserted in new-fangled gates, and departing trains are no longer brought in by Pannier tank engines (reminding one of puffing schoolboys) ready for genteel boarding twenty minutes early (the restaurant car chief steward standing on the platform doling out tickets for first, second and third sitting), Brunel's Paddington is still perhaps the most welcoming of the London termini, followed by the great contrasts of more modern King's Cross and a different splendour of Charing Cross.

Once Paddington veritably reeked of the seasons. The mechanical horses skilfully steered lines of trolleys packed with flowers and produce between guards' vans and parcels platform may have disappeared, but Chelsea Flower Show is just one seasonal event that brings in a noticeably different strand of people. Today many businessmen only work a four day week but those who still travel on Friday demonstrate it is dress-down day.

It is no longer Paddington for Birkenhead, Weymouth and many other destinations, yet most routes still served have special romance – though nothing more so than the line to the West Country. Incidentally, beyond Newton Abbot progress may be slower but a journey offers great geography and history all the way to Penzance. As a popular album was titled, it was indeed and still is the Great Way West.

SPRING EXPLORATION

SPRING WAS THE best time for exploring Britain by train. From home in Teignmouth I gradually covered all Devon and Cornwall on day trips. The Cornish ones involved starting before six in the morning using a Workmen's ticket to Plymouth (1/5d or today's 7p) and buying a day return on from there during the train's 20-minute layover.

My first trips away from home were largely based round places such as Bath and Cheltenham, where the family stayed while Dad attended the rotating conferences of the West Country Writers' Association. Much amusement was caused by long periods in the hotel lounge, regional timetables in hand, working out the next day's itinerary that allowed maximum route coverage with time to pop into a few towns and villages. Daylight was long and there were relatively few travellers before the holiday season (shorter in those days) got under way.

Then, when I could afford even an odd night away by myself, the north-eastward reach from home at Teignmouth was much extended, and eventually I covered most of Britain on trips of three or four long and somewhat exhausting days giving me a library of memories which I still delve into every day.

There were two favourite places on the train: in the front coach with the strap-controlled window down, and in the van with the guard. The former allowed one to see passengers waiting at stations and overhear conversation between staff and engine crew, especially on single lines where tokens were exchanged with the signalman.

Even on spring-time expresses, one usually had the front compartment to oneself, but one fellow passenger, a Welsh comedian, on an all-stations train, on his way to his father's funeral in Aberystwyth, used our strategic position to ensure we could continue talking without interruption. At a wayside station on the Mid-Wales line, on seeing a crowd waiting to go to market, he quickly took off his socks and hung them in the window. Rapidly he dishevelled himself and urged me to put my feet up on the opposite seat as untidily as I could. The rest of the two-coach train must have been crowded but only one woman tentatively opened our door… and quickly retreated. 'It worked,' said the comedian jovially.

It's an odd reflection on human nature that we nearly all seek solitude, one passenger per compartment being a familiar feature in the days before open seating, yet enjoy contacts with others. Though I loved my solitude, the most memorable of journeys were with others.

The guard's compartment was magic. Many country trains earned more from their parcel than passenger business. Especially true was this on the North Devon & Cornwall Junction Light Railway, where south of Petrockstow, one was invariably the sole passenger. But at Hatherleigh so many cases of rabbits strung up by their tails were loaded that every seat in the one-coach train other than mine accommodated them. Nasty smell.

Most guards, once over initial shyness, were happy to discuss seasonal patterns as well as what was currently in the van – and to point out farms and crops that were doing well or were in any way unusual. The guards were an odd collection of individuals, some thoughtful, some that just didn't seem to fit – men who wouldn't make it to driver and included failed signalmen such as one who had fallen asleep on night duty.

Mail bags, the railways' own parcels of all shapes and sizes, bicycles, a few groceries still distributed by train, notably Lyons cakes and ice cream, day-old chicks, calves, pigeons to be released at several stations, Covent Garden boxes (loaded or empty) and rabbit crates: at first they all looked higgledy-piggledy, but between stations they were reorganised so that those for the next stop could be quickly offloaded. 'It must produce a lot of revenue,' I said to one guard, who replied: 'It would do if the company [in BR days it was still invariably "the company"] weren't saddled with being common carriers. At some stations they have to order a taxi to deliver the ice cream. Ridiculous. The government expects us to pay but ties our hands'

Later, in Northumberland, I came across an example where a Lyons delivery van deposited ice cream at a parcels office whose guardian had to summon a taxi for delivery to a distant outpost, since being common carrier also applied to goods that never actually travelled by rail. Staff were often more enlightened than government, fond of imposing restrictions on supposedly commercially-run State institutions including to this day the Post Office.

The make up of the parcels and the aroma varied with the seasons, the scent of early flowers and fruit perhaps competing with the fresh droppings of a calf being delivered to improve the country's cattle – as, by encouraging movement, the railway enabled better human breeding. The elimination of the village idiot can be put down to the country railway.

Though the very earliest (and odd consignments produced away from traditional areas) went by passenger train, when intensively-grown crops were in full flush, flowers, fruit and vegetables required specials. The sound of broccoli specials running along the Teign Estuary could be heard almost continuously from my bedroom high above Teignmouth and I recall two ancient engines struggling up the bank from the bridge over the Tamar at Calstock to the main line at Bere Alston with a lengthy string of strawberry-filled vans, though, come to think of it, that was a mixed train with perhaps half a dozen people in the coach behind the engine.

After broccoli and strawberries came raspberries – specials from Fife being especially numerous. Then early potatoes, especially from Pembrokeshire, Channel Island tomatoes via Southampton and Weymouth – and the military-like operations of moving the plums from Evesham and Pershore. Sugar beet specials were common in East Anglia and Ireland, and even teazles were carried by the truck-full, notably in Somerset. Altogether it was big business.

One by one, all of this traffic eroded. A sad day for David & Charles was that on which BR ceased to be a general parcel carrier. Once we despatched all our books by passenger train. I could tell how well we were doing by looking at the loaded trucks nicknamed Brutes on Newton Abbot's up platform. The service was speedy and reliable, allowing us to head the table of publishers' rapid delivery.

Soon PLA (Passenger Luggage in Advance) was also abandoned. Passengers used to be able to pay extra for collection or delivery, or both. In the days when most boarding school children went by train (giving them the independence that they lack today), to save money most mums took their kid's trunk to the local station by car, frequently the family's second one such as a Morris Minor. The trunk would be delivered to the school at the other end.

For generations many holidaymakers sent their luggage PLA, necessitating special trains even on the Isle of Wight. Occasionally PLA went missing, the best-known example of which was at Scarborough. A whole van-full of it disappeared, with a major part of many families' wardrobes. In the 1930s, most men had only one suit. A harassed stationmaster was forced to pay emergency funds to tide visitors over until the whereabouts of the van was discovered, days later.

National newspapers only became country-wide in the railway age. Though their local distribution was centralised with road delivery long before that happened to the mail, the highest numbered platforms at Euston, rebuilt well into postwar times, were for mail and newspapers, and also intensively used for many years. Later they also came in useful for MotorRail in its declining years when whole trains had ceased and vehicles were carried in a few vans attached to passenger trains – mainly overnight ones. All have been lost; even the latter day Red Star parcels.

Today's sleeper arriving at Euston from the Highlands might carry a handful of parcels, such items as a freshly-caught wild salmon, but passenger trains are now almost exclusively for passengers. The rows of parcels trucks that mysteriously kept in line when drawn round the buffer stops of termini are but a memory, along with rows of porters and their trolleys competing to earn the best tips, wheel tappers, and gas being pumped into the restaurant car's kitchen (a red flag sticking out to warn it shouldn't be moved). No longer can one tell the character of the crops of different valleys at important stations and junctions. In behaviour and appearance even humans have become more standardised, passengers arriving from 'posh' West Country places no longer readily distinguishable from those from the South Wales valleys.

Back to parcels. The big decision facing senders used to be 'Passenger or Freight?' Both could be collected or delivered at the parcels office, but there was a huge difference in cost, speed and risk. Parcels might arrive by any passenger train; goods parcels only came in the daily station truck, a loose-coupled van usually toward the middle of a goods

train which came jerkily to a standstill not too far from the parcels office. Though the parcels clerk might offer advice, the choice was up to the sender. Usually only well-padded heavy, sturdy, non-perishable items arrived by the station truck. In the days when everything in the valley or hill-top town arrived by train, one item that almost certainly came goods rather than passenger was the kitchen sink.

There were naturally many other aspects to touring Britain by train. The spring landscape was gorgeous. In the steam age when embankments were still scythed by hand and the vegetation burned, usually in July, wild flowers abounded alongside the track. Many trees were in flower but their vegetation not yet thick enough to obscure the view beside the numerous rivers where trains were in a world of their own, well away from parallel roads. How I loved those river scenes, and the way that the track had been laid with the maximum straight lengths between curves. Yet better still were the lines that ran alongside lakes such as at Bala in North Wales and Bassenthwaite near Keswick. Sea, mountain and moor; each held their different charms. We can still enjoy all three in a single journey on the West Highland Line

When driving in convoys on crowded roads, I look enviously at the route of the old Great Western branch from Bala to Blaenau Ffestiniog, reliving my memory of train journeys and how grateful I am to be born early enough to experience them. Wherever one went, even in flat Lincolnshire, the land was full of interest seen from a different perspective.

In later years, the early Diesel units allowed the front-seat passengers to share the driver's view, tracing the progress of water courses, and seeing level crossing gates opening − sometimes several sets of them – just ahead of us, the signalmen delaying stopping road traffic till the last moment. The railway didn't usually show off towns to the best advantage, though bird's eye views such as of Durham and Truro have always been notable, it invariably made the most of the countryside, from farmsteads to bubbling streams cutting their course downhill and becoming more forceful as they were joined by tributaries, to the dramatic landscape and engineering achievements of the Long Drag, the Settle & Carlisle. Or again, and from estuaries lake-like at high tide and full of feeding birds at low, to the chalk hills of the Weald.

When I scan each new timetable, automatically I conjure up scenes from different routes – of branches long closed as well as the huge legacy still there to enjoy, though on today's short, packed trains it is hard to enjoy solitude, and views are obstructed from many seats.

But, then, who wants to look out of the window asked Virgin's Branson, boasting about plans for mini-screens to keep West Coast passengers happy. 'See Britain by Rail' is distinctively yesterday's slogan, though substantial numbers do in fact still do just that, and certainly more ramblers than ever use trains to get them into walking country, and have greatly helped swell the passenger numbers on the Settle & Carlisle among other lines.

All this almost ignores the interest in the railway itself: its operation, motive power and staff, and the architecture bequeathed by the original companies that built them. On the former Furness lines, look out for the station seats, their cast-iron ends with a motif featuring red squirrels, one of whose remaining English enclaves is the south west Lake District. On the London & South Western, look out for the gable-ended station houses. They were built over half a century as the line to North Cornwall was steadily extended to link with the pioneer little Bodmin & Wadebridge, bought as it happens illegally by the South Western when its own system scarcely reached Basingstoke.

Travellers on the ball consulting their timetable knew where trains would 'cross' (pass each other at stations on single lines), their watches telling them if there'd be time to stroll on the platform. The first train in was usually the last to leave. Junctions held a particular fascination, with refreshment rooms even at places like Moat Lane Junction and Dovey Junction on the route from Shrewsbury to Aberystwyth: occasionally there was time to dash to one even if one were not changing. If you were really in the know, you could also count on a stroll where the engine took on water, something once so common, but on the national system long confined to steam specials, when the Fire Service is often brought in to help.

Railway exploration, especially in spring, was the joy of my life. The only disappointment was that the system eventually shrunk so rapidly that one couldn't possibly use every route before it was pruned. An especial sorrow is that I never travelled on the Midland & Great Northern Joint line, though a friend taking me out by car for a day called in at several stations including the all-important Melton Constable and Norwich's second station, a single line terminus at the end of the branch line from it.

That, like the other two joint routes, the Somerset & Dorset and the Cheshire Lines, not merely opened a different territory but naturally held strong railway interest in the Grouping Era. Indeed, even the penetrating lines of the big four were fascinating: The LMS in

Central and South Wales, the LNER on the west coast, the SR at Bodmin & Wadebridge, and the GWR's ex-Midland & South West Junction down to Winchester. Though the minor, mainly terminal, stations at the end of the penetrating lines remarkably held on until nationalisation, 'rationalisation' then became the flavour of the day. Launceston, Barnstaple, Bath, Reading, Oxford, Swansea and Perth among others lost their secondary stations. Some of these underdog termini took some finding. Even those living nearby didn't help much in my search for Bristol St Philip's, a single wooden-sleeper platform used by a handful of weekday trains to Bath Green Park and a single evening one to Yate.

Yet the individual character of the original owners surprisingly survives even in different ownership such as Bath Green Park as a Sainsbury's. This is especially true in Scotland where the different approach to creating a railway between say the Caledonian and the North British remains very evident.

The joy of exploring Britain by train is many faceted. The shame is that there are now so few restaurant cars offering good wine and food further to enhance the pleasure.

EXCURSION

HAPPY MEMORIES. NEAT little girls and dishevelled boys pouring out of the station side entrance on their Sunday School outing eager to get to the beach. The sound of merriment rising from the sands close to the railway station at places such as Goodrington and Barry Island. The latter was one of several places where excursion train drivers had sufficient mid-day break to join their families beside the sea.

Again, wide-eyed children enjoying a pantomime thanks to an affordable excursion train. Whole families taking a last trip at the end of the season making the most of Blackpool Illuminations and everything else Britain's most popular resort had to offer. School parties on trips selected from the 'educational excursions' programme seeing chocolate made at Bourneville or enjoying a short Thames boat trip, having first walked wondrously from the train to Windsor Castle.

Boys of all ages cheering their football teams at distant places they never thought it would be in their power to reach.

Elderly folk able to ring the changes of a resort in which to spend the afternoon. Flower lovers arriving by the trainful for the pleasures of Southport Flower Show, the world's largest. Back to children: grammar school kids enjoying an escorted full-day visit to the Festival of Britain, as so many of their great, great grandparents had managed to make an epoch-making trip to the Great Exhibition a century earlier (after pawning their watches). The Great Exhibition was the first event to be enjoyed by people of all classes from many parts of the country. Those from Furness travelled by steamer from Piel Pier to join a train at Morecambe.

The excursion train was truly revolutionary. Full-day, half-day and evening excursions made travel possible in a way that even third class or Parliamentary services didn't. Fares could be so cheap that a bus trip back from the station to home at the day's end might be the more expensive. In the 1930s for as little as 3s 6d Birmingham folk could savour the joys of Weston-super-Mare or a choice of East Coast resorts.

Perhaps nothing better emphasises the seasonal nature of railways and indeed the British life they served and developed better than the excursion train. It was quickly realised that carrying hundreds or thousands cheaply on special trains opened up a whole new source of business. Pragmatically anything that created a sufficient pool of traffic could and would be exploited, the best times for making money being at spring weekends when fine weather released a pent-up demand to be out and about, throughout the summer and on special occasions not the least of which used to be Christmas. But throughout the year local events could be put to profit and the needs of clubs and societies exploited.

Pragmatic indeed was what probably the first excursion run specifically for a public event on 13 April 1840. H Kyde, superintendent of the tiny, isolated Bodmin & Wadebridge, whose main source of revenue was carrying sea sand rich in lime for farmers, ran a train to enable bloodthirsty locals to view a public execution. The carriages were parked on an embankment, giving a bird's eye view of the gallows outside Bodmin jail.

We do not know for sure which was the very earliest excursion train. But starting a long tradition of excursions serving religion, as early as 1838 the Whitby & Pickering ran one in connection with a bazaar to raise church funds. Advertising stressed: 'The train will leave at five o'clock in the morning, and parties will have to be wide awake at an early hour, or they will suffer disappointment. Promptitude on the part of the railways calls for the same from the passengers.'

In the early days most early excursions were tied to a specific organisation, many linked to the Temperance Movement. One on the pioneer West Cornwall – incorporating the first part of the route of the GWR's Penzance mainline to be built – needed seventy six mineral trucks pulled by three engines to carry members of the Camborne Temperance Society to Hayle. The teetotallers sang

> Happy Camborne, happy Camborne
> Where the railway is so near;
> And the engine shows how water
> Can accomplish more than beer.

And when the engine broke down outside a cider orchard, they scrambled up the trees and left them fruitless.

Temperance was the driving force behind Thomas Cook, founder of the iconic travel company. It was not until 1841 that he ran his first excursion, so by no means the first ever as has often been wrongly said. Even the claim that it was the first publicly-advertised one doesn't hold up. What was different and was the foundation stone of the travel empire, is that it was the first organised and accompanied by an outside intermediary. We don't know on what terms the Midland Counties Railway agreed to run the train, but it is likely that Cook took an entrepreneural risk. He must have been relieved as well as ecstatic when 570 people crowded onto the platform at Leicester having paid a shilling for the return journey to Loughborough, eleven miles away, for a temperance rally. Space on the trains of nine open and seatless 'tubs' was appreciably cheaper than the third class fare.

Commercial operators, from Thomas Cook on a grand scale to I myself organising events such as carrying 500 on day trips from London to St Michael's Mount near Penzance for cream teas, played a significant role. The train journey was then often part of an inclusive tour – what for longer holidays developed into the package deal. In railway terminology a train run for another sponsor became a charter. Yet the vast majority of excursions were organised by the railways themselves, and again a large proportion of them were to exploit attractions on a seasonal basis.

The excursion officer or manager was an important member of the top team at district offices. He decided what event might justify an excursion, worked out a schedule with the operating people, set the fares and not least undertook extensive advertising. That involved prodigious preparation of individual posters, handbills and booklets. Though by then it had become a high-class printing works, when I bought the Plymouth firm of Latimer Trend, there was still extensive railway work and a marvellous array of wooden block type for large-print poster headings. It had earlier claimed to be a 'general and railway' printer. For many years there was also regular advertising in local papers.

Early in history, 'excursion' also included cheap fares by ordinary train, and the difference between specials and regular service trains narrowed, extra demand leading to many regular trains having to run in several parts. The excursion manager included all in his orbit. Even on ordinary trains the cheap tickets were tightly regulated so as not to be available to broader traffic. For example, it was illegal to dash from a train at an intermediate station to buy another cheap ticket, making a longer journey cheaper than the advertised fare for it.

Bargain fares were for just between the stations for which they were advertised. So alighting at an earlier destination than you booked for could involve a surcharge greater than the original fare. After a publicised complaint, one general manager defended his company's policy in a letter to *The Times* saying it was fraudulent for anyone not to stick to the terms of the special offer – inflexibility we now accept when making cheap train or air bookings. Advertisements for many excursions made the point: 'No luggage allowed.'

Though in our time excursion trains were made up of standard stock and often had a buffet, in the early days only the worst accommodation was provided. When a coroner recorded that a third-class passenger in an open truck on an ordinary Great Western train had died of exposure without feeling the need to make further comment, we can only imagine what it must have been like on some of the earliest long-distance excursions involving very early starts and late returns, a day stretching to thirty or more hours. On some to distant parts, the return was on a separate day – or out and back by successive nights, leaving no opportunity for real sleep.

'The impropriety of running excursion trains at all is manifest' was the startling opening comment by the respected Railway Inspector Col Yolland reporting on an accident that befell a Manchester to Scarborough excursion. At which point let it be said that overall surprisingly few people were killed in accidents to excursion trains, but the handful we'll now look at revealed shocking laxity. Much thin ice must have been skated. And as it happens, several of these accidents paved the way for vital basic safety improvements.

Col Yolland went on to qualify his remarks on the heavily-laden excursion from Manchester on the Lancashire & Yorkshire in 1860: 'if a company has not the means of putting efficient men in charge of them, as they frequently become, from the low fares which the public are enabled to travel in them, exceedingly heavy and unmanageable… much more difficult to drive.' He added that the one brakevan for eight carriages was quite inadequate.

Eighty excursionists died in what was then the worst accident on railways in the British Isles. On 12 June 1889, the fated train was on its way from Armagh to Warrenpoint in Northern Ireland, killing two more than the Taybridge disaster when staff and all passengers lost their lives. What especially hurt was that the eighty killed included many children on their annual treat, Armagh's Methodist Sunday School outing to the sea. The engine stalled on the stiff gradient out of Armagh, and the inspector in charge ordered that the train should be divided. With inadequate precautions, the last ten vehicles rolled away down the incline and collided with a regular following train. No accident had a greater influence on later safety and signalling, the compulsory use of a continuous automatic brake being the most significant. The government, in the days of laissez-faire, loath to intervene in private business, was forced into action.

The public were even more outraged by the head-on crash near Radstock on the single line Somerset & Dorset on 7 August 1876. Though only thirteen people were killed, what was revealed was the line's 'state of positive disorganisation': an over-stretched railway, with tired and even illiterate staff taking short cuts, and a key signalman refusing to answer a telegraph enquiry sensibly. This accident also emphasised the liability the LSWR and Midland had taken on by snatching ownership of the S&D while talks were being held with the Great Western. Edward Tyler's famous electric token system, was the chief, if not only result. On all routes, it soon became obligatory for drivers on a single line not to proceed until they had possession of the one and only token in circulation.

Yet only one other accident in England and Wales involving an excursion happened between 1870 and 1914, when millions were carried cheaply to parts of the country they never expected to visit. That one was at the small town of Welshampton on the Welsh border on 11 June 1897. The enquiry found that the track was defective and not up to the speed that the Cambrian was operating at, though for generations local company loyalty insisted it was actually the poor state of the four-wheeled Lancashire & Yorkshire brakevan that ran roughly.

The Holidays with Pay Act 1948, giving all workers a statutory right to a minimum paid week a year, rising to two weeks, made little immediate difference to the numbers staying away from home. A 1949 survey found that 23 per cent of the population went nowhere even on a day trip, and many of those hadn't been anywhere for 'many years'. But there was a greater impact on day trips. Over half of those not taking a proper holiday went on at least one excursion. Most who went away stayed only for a week, so giving them time for an excursion… or an extra one if they were already excursionists.

Old habits died hard. Many who stayed away did so with family or friends, and both those who paid to stay away and excursionists mainly went to the traditional haunts such as Rhyl, Blackpool, Great Yarmouth and Weston-Super-Mare, or made for a nearer seaside Working Men's Club. Holiday camps were in their infancy and, while bus competition had made serious inroads, on a hot day in early June 1950, there was still good-natured 'pandemonium', as a ticket collector called it, at Newcastle Central, where from noon till 4.00pm a four-deep queue snaked its way toward a succession of trains for the nearby seaside.

Conversations and habits were very working class, people liking being en masse. A rising phenomena was the increasing popularity of smaller, less brash resorts, such as in Devon and Cornwall and steadily, and as families became smaller, solitude and walking became widely valued. When the Peak District became Britain's first National

Park, visitor numbers were small and very few walked. How that has changed.

As remarked at the beginning of the chapter on summer Saturdays, the West Country also gained popularity because going there was seen as 'adventurous'. Eventually the love of being on one's own totally changed the holiday map and railway timetable. However, in 1950 three million went to Blackpool for the illuminations, restored in 1949, and Morecambe and others were putting on their less spectacular but attractive light shows pulling in popular crowds. Where the big resorts gained especially in pre-motoring times was in organising fun and providing indoor attractions for rainy days.

In Ireland an exceptionally higher proportion of passengers travelled by special train, including emigration specials after the potato famine. Great was the emotion as relatives said farewell, in most cases never to meet again. For many of the emigrants, it was their only long-distance journey on home soil. The same was true in Cornwall after the 1870 collapse of mining.

Irish excursions largely involved Sunday pilgrimages, successive trains on the same route following each other at roughly the same distance apart as they resumed after pausing at different stations for morning Mass. Traffic was especially heavy at Claremorris where, within an hour, half a dozen trains might arrive from different directions.

Race specials were another Irish speciality, as were complicated special workings delivering and collecting the horses to venues such as the Curragh with its special station for race traffic.

On both sides of the Irish Sea, excursions became more complex and hybrid. For instance, the Irish *Radio Train,* with meal service for all, though obviously an excursion, became a timetabled feature to Killarney and other resorts on different dates.

Both before and after World War Two, land cruise trains were popular, offering intriguing single-day circular tours in style, occasionally with nights away. Now only trains such as the privately-owned *Orient Express* and *Royal Scotsman* do such tours and today's tight rolling stock limitations almost prevent railway-run excursions and severely limit charters.

While mass excursionists have always been unpopular in a few 'select' resorts, more fears were aroused when rumours circulated that special cheap trains might be abolished. In the larger resorts, many businesses became highly dependent on trippers who often outnumbered staying guests. For the most part the railways knew they were onto a good thing and rumours were unfounded.

Now an eclectic selection of examples of the scale of excursion traffic over the years:

June **1843**. 3,000 passengers returned to Manchester in 62 carriages after an excursion to Alderley, where the 'Edge' rises sharply from the Cheshire plain. Alderley's population was then less than a thousand (Wilmslow's less than 4,000), and such excursions were used to stimulate interest in moving out of the city, allowing a period of free travel to those who built houses.

Easter Monday **1844** was the day when the aristocrats of Brighton must have feared – correctly as it proved – that their elite world was coming to an end. The first excursion arrived from London, a train of forty five short open carriages taking 4½ hours to cover the 50½ miles from London Bridge. Already an annual season ticket was offered at £50; Sunday excursions cost 5s. A revolution was unleashed which quickly made Queen Victoria decide never to revisit the town.

August **1847**, the first excursion reached Windermere, fulfilling Wordsworth's fears that the railway's arrival would spoil the lake's magic. The number of excursionists rose rapidly, 8,000 arriving on Whit Monday 1883. The railway also brought the wealthy, many of whom built lavish homes. When the branch was reduced to single track in 1973, excursionists detrained into a fleet of road coaches at Oxenholme

1848. The Lancashire & Yorkshire played the market. From Mumps, Oldham, an excursion ticket to Blackpool cost men 1s 6d but women only 1s. When it was suspected that men were dressing as women, the superintendent who came with four inspectors to investigate was overwhelmed by the rush of impatient passengers, trampled on, and became unconscious.

July **1852** saw the first excursion from London to the West Country, allowing a week in a choice of resorts. The fare to Plymouth was just £1. Some 1,500 passengers were carried in thirty three carriages, the train being too long for any platform. The journey time was an astonishing 13½ hours. Even the regular train that became known as the Plymouth Cheap, at Parliamentary fares, was overtaken en route by more costly expresses.

By **1865,** when excursions ran from London to most South Coast resorts, exceptional value of 2s 6d to Whitstable, and 4s 6d to Herne Bay by covered carriage, was due to intense competition between the South Eastern and Chatham, which later joined forces.

1866 saw the doubling of the loop line serving Weston-Super-Mare to carry 'such numbers of excursionists as nevertheless seem surprising at other places', the fare from Bristol being 1s 6d. In the 'excursion hall' outside the improved station, tea cost 1½d, or could be made free by travellers carrying their own ingredients. Weston was among the places successfully resisting the railway in the first place, and was initially connected by a horse-powered branch at right angles to the mainline. As at so many other places, the peak was reached on a Sunday afternoon in 1939: 38,000. The four-platform Locking Road built for excursions proved handy as summer Saturday business reached its later peak, but has long been but a memory.

On 28 July **1870**, the first train across the giant viaduct over the Solway Firth was an excursion allowing people from Aspatria to the south to attend the Dumfries Agricultural Show. Partly because the Firth had been such an historic separation, the expensive line never lived up to expectation and, having been closed as unsafe in 1921, proved even more difficult and costly to demolish in the 1930s.

1885 saw 3–4,000 Preston people who paid 3s arrive in 'peaceful' Keswick one Sunday, giving the railway company a shock as it was keen to see the town keep its reputation for discerning passengers. 'The Board... do not see how excursion traffic can be avoided, but the secretary is instructed not to promote such traffic by Special Train.' Until the 1950s a timetabled double-headed Sunday excursion with buffet from the East Coast via Barnard Castle took almost an hour to shunt and stable at Keswick, ready for the evening return.

In **1892**, it was noted that trains for trippers brought Hunstanton 'hundreds at a time from Cambridgeshire, Lincolnshire and elsewhere', while 1905 saw restaurant car excursions from Liverpool Street for golfers.

In **1905**, excursions from a dozen places as far away as Lincoln, Liverpool and Bradford dropped their passengers at Newington on the short Hull avoiding line, also mentioned in the chapter on summer Saturdays. Hull's giant pleasure fair was held nearby each autumn.

On August Bank Holiday **1907**, six trains were needed to sweep up all the excursionists who presented themselves at Liverpool Street for a half-day excursion to Skegness. The total number of excursionists taken to the resort that year was 321,000, which grew two and a half times until war interrupted things in 1914.

In the **1920s**, for a bargain 2s 11d (only 14½p in today's money), an excursion ran 'along the backbone of England' on the Settle & Carlisle from Leeds and Bradford, returning via Shap and Ingleton.

In the **1930s**, up to 20,000 excursionists were carried up the first part of the Plymouth-Launceston branch, mainly to stations between Plym Bridge Platform and Yelverton, the latter being as far as the occasional 4-6-0 tender engine was allowed. After the war, 2,000 was rarely exceeded, though it reached 8,000 on occasional Easter and Whit Bank Holidays. While West Country people were ahead of the masses in the industrial North in enjoying good scenery and walking, in real summer the beach was the automatic choice, the most popular destination by train for Plymothians being Goodrington Sands, requiring reversal at Newton Abbot. There used also to be a through excursion from Ilfracombe to Bude and vice versa on alternate summer Sundays, the two crossing at Petrockstowe where the number of passengers must have been greater than passing through for the rest of the fortnight. Reversal was necessary at Barnstaple Junction and Halwill Junction.

On Sundays in the **1930s**, the large circulating area within Scarborough's excursion station was filled with thousands waiting for their return trains – up to ten an hour (including a few from the main station) running between 7 and 10.00pm. Evening excursions arrived between 6 and 7.30, departing between 10.15 and 11.25, allowing a few hours beside the sea for 2s or 3s. On fine Sundays four of five trains ran from Leeds alone.

In **1937**, the Southern ran 1,023 race and 259 football specials, still dwarfed by 1,480 extra boat trains. Eventually 'excursions' to the resorts were almost always by ordinary trains, frequently in several parts. Extra traffic of all kinds was always a feature of railways south of the Thames, whose reputation for speed and punctuality was – and still remains – far below that of routes to the west and north.

In the **1950s**, up to 8,000 passengers travelled on Sunday early afternoon relief services just between Exeter St Thomas and Dawlish Warren. As most Devon people became car owners their experience would become quite different.

RESTAURANT CARS

RESTAURANT CAR MEALS were usually a delight. Almost weekly for many years, I travelled to London from Devon, and greatly enjoyed breakfasts, lunches, afternoon teas and dinners. Much of the time lunches and dinners were four-course affairs with a tasty fish course. Not only were the meals of the highest quality at reasonable prices but, in the days of compartments, the open restaurant car offered a better view – and there was a friendly almost club-like atmosphere, especially among regulars and the crews.

Not always did everything go smoothly and I recall a few ugly moments, but generally expectations were more than met. Wines were of the highest order, especially when a large quantity was discovered hidden away in the centralised catering department at St Pancras (which also supplied the Transport Hotels) and rare vintages were sold off cheap.

The scenery (see 'A Country Journey like no Other', page 60) was also to dream about, especially sun rising out of the winter sea between Teignmouth and Dawlish as one tucked into porridge, though once that had to be replaced after drops of salt water from a wave breaking over the train came through a crack in the window.

My experience, starting before the war, included journeys in all parts of the country with their strong regional variations in the restaurant cars themselves as well as the fare they served. High tea was naturally a speciality in Scotland: a full afternoon tea preceded by fish and chips or meat. However, the average Scottish standard was below that in most of England.

Considering the general comfort of its seating, Great Western restaurant cars were not especially good, but one could always round off a main meal with cheese and the marvellous Huntley & Palmer Great Western assorted biscuits... hoping that favourites (notably crunchy breakfast biscuits) hadn't already disappeared from the circulating tin.

The most comfortable cars were on the LMS/London Midland, including triple sets with separate first-class and third-class cars on either side of the kitchen car. There were also a few single-cars with the kitchen sandwiched between first and third-class. One such was used on the LNER's West Highland line, where the train connected with ferries that also had their separate dining saloons. With Western Isles passengers dominating, demand was thin and so little food was carried that any surge meant it ran out. I was once turned away from this vehicle by the crew tucking into their lunch saying 'No food left'.

More happily, back on the LMS, I recall a generous if somewhat stodgy afternoon tea served in an ex-Midland wood-panelled car with bow shaped ends on the Oban route. On both routes to the West Coast, at least one had a grand view of extraordinarily vibrant scenery. And these were lines where the appearance of the landscape and the amount of water gushing down waterfalls, the track sometimes splitting them into two, very much depended on the time of year. From May to September travellers included many anxious to point out the changing features, frisky lambs being early in the year and bright rowanberries later. The same was true of the *Thames-Clyde* and *Waverley* expresses over the Settle & Carlisle or Long Drag, the preferred route to Scotland for lovers of mountain scenery, again best seen from the restaurant car. Over the years I ate lunch on a number of occasions on this route, including on diverted and special services but, while I record the scenery and the company, the food comes last in my memory. Occasional rainbows made greater impressions.

Other oddities included claustrophobically-dislikeable 'Tavern' cars with their mock olde-worlde brick covering the whole exterior with no space for windows. They were among the inventions of the Southern's controversial Bullied. On other former Southern routes, the practice of leasing catering to the Pullman Company continued well after the end of war in 1945. The single Pullman fitted untidily into the train profile. Service levels on these cars, as so much else about the railways south of the Thames, disappointed.

The separate Pullman car trains where you ate at your seat were quite different, the updated all-Pullman *Golden Arrow* maintaining high standards for cross-channel ferries until finally beaten by air competition in 1957.

The last all-Pullman south of the Thames was the *Brighton Belle* which shuttled to and forth in just an hour several times a day. Its standards suffered somewhat in later years and many older readers may remember Sir Lawrence Olivier, protesting about the withdrawal of kippers from the breakfast menu. When he was successful in having them reinstated, he declined one on his next morning journey and, when interviewed, said it was the principle of choice that mattered.

The Western Region's Blue Pullmans and a new set of Pullmans led by the *Manchester Pullman* had a short heyday, superseded by the HSTs and electric rolling stock also using Mark 3 coaches. That spelt not only the end of Gold Star dinners offering even more luxury on trains such as the *Golden Hind* from Paddington to the West, but the end of restaurant cars on cross-country routes.

As guest at a small get-together organised by the South West Transport Users' Consultative Council, the chairman unexpectedly asked me to start off a discussion, so hastily I expressed disappointment about the ending of good meals on cross-country trains and said that as a result I had started driving on trips to Glasgow and Edinburgh. The roads including much motorway were not busy in those days, and there was time to slip into a nearby pub for lunch.

'My dear sir,' interjected a short, seemingly patronising man. 'What would your accountant say to the cost of driving a Cortina just for yourself?' Titters. 'Oh, that obviously means what you drive costs even more. Has your accountant ever worked out the relative costs?'

To which I replied in the same tone: 'My dear sir, I don't care a toss what my accountant thinks. What matters is that I get to Scotland in good fettle to sign up authors and make sales that render transport costs irrelevant.'

We agreed to differ, and it was only after we met in the gents and he told me he was sure I was sincere, and I said likewise, that I realised that he was Robert Reid, the supremo of British Railways, the first of the two successive heads of the same name as chance had it. Very much a back office worker, when he travelled by HST, it was in one of two Executive Cars that, given notice and at a high cost, could be included in the set to allow privacy. It was perhaps the start of hiding away from customers that has become too fashionable, today's station managers endlessly sitting over their computers and seldom venturing out onto platforms on public view as did the old stationmasters, often especially welcoming business travellers and encouraging them to use the restaurant car.

When originally planned, the HSTs were to have two separate catering vehicles, a restaurant in first-class and buffet in standard-class. Because of changing public tastes, and to be fair also quicker journey times, what actually emerged was a single catering vehicle with long buffet, kitchen and a comfortable 17-seater restaurant.

Cross-country trains from the west to the north and Scotland, had been mainly controlled, as were the Paddington services, from Plymouth, where the functionary known as the Circuit Manager expected the highest standard and routinely monitored things. He engaged good staff by making a timely bid to get the pick of high school boys (who were not heading on to university) from Plymouth and Devonport. He wouldn't however entertain women. Restaurant cars were man's work, and he had sufficient independence to maintain this even when women waiters appeared on other routes. Because of the rich territory served, there was never a shortage of staff on the Western.

In passing, most early immigrants came from the West Indies, catching their first glimpse of the country that was to become their family home on the boat train journey including the GW's named Ocean Saloons from Plymouth to Paddington and that was the last of the London terminals that, in the language of the day, 'needed' to employ them.

The Circuit Manager had a discretionary entertainment allowance, and on several occasions I was invited to a free meal, or told my bill would be taken care of when I finished one. Once that was a luxury tea with Welsh Rarebit as well as the usual bread and butter with jam, sandwiches and cake and, since on this occasion I was entertaining two directors after a board meeting, it included a bottle of champagne. The journey was on the short-lived *West Country Pullman* on its return trip to London from Paignton via Bristol and – where remaining seats were filled – Bath.

It was always possible to reserve on busy trains, and on quiet trains one might spend the entire journey in the restaurant car with its first-class seating even if one were travelling standard.

The Plymouth-based Circuit Manager and his team, including some colourful individuals who when they saw the writing on the wall set up their own businesses, and did their best to maintain standards with the more limited HST facilities. For some time a number of tables in the adjoining first-class coach – referred to as the 'top car' – were also laid up. The food remained good as did the patronage especially for breakfast on popular businessmen's trains. Increasingly lunch was seen as a time for a sandwich and a beer, and the number of trains offering full lunch declined.

It now comes as a surprise to realise that until well into nationalised (post-1948) days the choice on most services had been a full meal or nothing. Though there had been some pioneer buffets in the 1930s, they didn't catch on, so even morning coffee and biscuits remained a set thing (often in several sittings) in the restaurant car. To accommodate the maximum number of passengers, on summer Saturdays West Country trains served up to six sittings of a two-course affair, cold meat and a pudding.

Though crews happily heated babies' bottles, something you don't see mums going to the buffet to have done today, only occasional one-off offerings might be made along the train by otherwise idle staff. The last time I remember that was on the *Pines Express* out of Bath toward Bournemouth when a pair of waiters visited our compartment, one offering a napkin and collecting the money, the other handing a generous ice-cream wafer. It was also on the last part of the Bournemouth-bound *Pines Express* that the chef threw out a bone to a dog who had grown used to waiting for it. On the final trip, before the *Pines* was diverted via Reading and Basingstoke, the ceremonial throwing out of the bone became the stuff of headlines.

When it was full service or nothing, restaurant cars ran on an extraordinarily wide range of routes, but often for only part of the journey. To keep costs down, on the Far North line, for example, you ate early going north and late coming south after cars had been transferred between trains at The Mound or Helmsdale. It was Achnasheen for the one daily pair of trains with meal service on the Kyle of Lochalsh line. In Devon in summer before the war, even South Molton was transfer point for a midday restaurant car.

Though looking after passengers was seen as worth subsidising, costs were always a constraint. So only on summer Saturdays did a Southern Railway/Region restaurant car venture beyond Exeter Central. And, again especially in Scotland, there were various attempts at providing cheaper and more contemporary-feeling griddle and brasserie cars before the retreat to buffet or trolley service only.

Privatisation brought mixed fortunes. The Great Western started well, but the original franchise owners who had real railway experience were tempted to sell out. Since then there's been a steady downhill story in general morale and performance. At the time of writing, only two restaurant cars leave Paddington a day, both bound for Plymouth. A Travelling Chef will cook a traditional railway breakfast fry-up at a bargain price on some trains but, like trolley service, it's a bit unpredictable. Now First Great Western are even taking off most buffets, so there will only be a trolley.

GNER (Great Northern & Eastern) started well on the East Coast, and steadily did better, with excellent restaurant cars on most of an increasing number of trains. GNER meals were a real treat, especially breakfast through the Pass of Drumochter and lunch along the Northumberland coast past Holy Island. But by now, universally in the British Isles, restaurant cars had become a Monday–Friday affair mainly aimed at the business market. The franchise was terminated because of financial problems with Sea Containers, the owning company. National who won it over with over-optimistic traffic expectations and inflated self-confidence, met problems and cut virtually all the restaurants and then had its franchise also halted. The service, still without restaurant cars, is now temporarily re-nationalised.

It seems the government is only interested in what it can get out of franchises, with little thought to overall standards and, after the failure of two successive East Coast ones, the whole system is severely criticised. Certainly short, competitive franchises, with frequent changes of operator, doesn't encourage taking the longer view. Even when provision of restaurant cars has been included in franchise offers, it doesn't seem to have been enforced.

Virgin's longer franchise on the West Coast route has enabled a more balanced view to be taken, and there are again a handful of full restaurant cars, while all first-class passengers are entitled to a full breakfast… though mainly served on trains where only astonishingly high fares are available. Virgin lost its own Cross Country franchise where, except for first-class passengers served at their seats in core hours, a useful lunch box was handed out, and drinks served from 'the shop'. Its successor's first act was to abolish the shop to allow more seating. Trolley service can be good, but availability is sketchy.

After privatisation the service from Liverpool Street to Norwich still offered good meals, during which one could enjoy the different East Anglian scenery with some surprising gradients, and severe speed restrictions round curves at the top of estuaries.

Happily ScotRail still includes a lounge car on their sleepers, one's enjoyment perhaps being dependent on the time of year, for in summer daylight in the north is long and darkness comes soon in winter.

For the most part eating on trains now means at best fast food or less at the bar or less from a trolley. For afternoon tea you have to turn to one of the steam railways and, for the broader luxury we once took everyday for granted, to the likes of the *Orient Express*.

Outside London, railway hotels were the best in the country. Even in the capital, they were fine extensions of the stations, seen by Brunel and others as a natural ancillary for travellers. Glasgow had three first class railway hotels. The rival companies sent their hotel committees on continental tours to select the best ideas and practices. In the Scottish countryside, Gleneagles and Turnberry were destinations in themselves. Outstanding décor, beautiful gardens, the most comfortable beds and high service is what one also remembers about the English 'resort' hotels such as Tregenna Castle at St Ives and the Welcome at Stratford-upon-Avon. Some visitors reached the latter, LMS owned, by an early rail-road vehicle.

Maggie Thatcher didn't agree with Brunel and the Transport Hotels were sold off in her reign. It was the most reckless as well as first piece of privatisation with silly rules. For example, hotels were sold in units of eight, some resold within weeks at double the price paid. A management buy-out was sneered at.

Almost all the hotels deteriorated shockingly, and at some the access to stations was blocked. Most departure monitors were removed. A few hotels have happily been redeveloped and refurbished, but in very few places are they now the automatic quality choice for the discerning. As with restaurant cars, memories of what things were like lingered on for older people. Little do younger business executives travelling around Britain know what they missed.

SUMMER

SUMMER SATURDAYS

A very special atmosphere of expectation pervaded West Country stations and the holiday resorts on summer Friday evenings. All kinds of railway staff and hoteliers, restaurateurs, taxi drivers, bankers and even telephone operators, prepared, wondering what joys or problems the morrow would bring. For example, would the first trains make their way punctually in the small hours, disgorging crowds who might wake up locals by joyfully singing while still on the station platform before moving on to restaurants serving an early leisurely breakfast to those who wouldn't be welcomed in their guest houses or B&Bs till much later? How big would the cash takings be? Water usage, deck-chair receipts, sales of postcards, cream for posting home and souvenirs: they all depended on the size of the crowds.

Meanwhile, at many cities people were excitedly setting out. 'Many of those who departed throughout the night were in a jolly mood, and singing, accompanied by the music of accordions, took the tedium out of the waiting period,' said the *Coventry Telegraph* of the last Friday/Saturday in July 1953. It added that about 25,000, the same as the year before, had left on long-distance journeys during the rush period. 'There was a smooth system of queuing outside the station entrance. As each new train came into the station, its queue was admitted in an orderly crocodile to the platform.'

Summer Saturdays on the railways were both a great business and sporting event, making newspaper headlines. Before the war, and again from the late 1940s, the Saturday timetables of some routes had their separate and fascinating pages. Not only the crowds actually on their way to and from holiday, but whole industries were dependent on each day's performance, especially in the 1950s, also studied and often photographed by thousands of railway enthusiasts around the country.

At remoter resorts, especially in the West Country, the big question was always how well, or even how many hours late, overnight trains were arriving on Saturday mornings. Major delays caused havoc, especially when that meant that the return workings couldn't start on time. Saturday breakfast times might then bring a build-up of returning visitors not allowed to enter the station – even if it were raining. On the worst days, such were the crowds filling station approaches that taxis had to drop their passengers and luggage on a busy road.

There is natural interest or satisfaction when a system of any kind fully comes into its own, with no capacity wasted. That was undoubtedly true on many branch lines as well as mainlines. Every carriage, every locomotive and eventually every siding, was pressed into service. Ten-coupled goods engines were used on passenger trains.

Especially in the mid-1950s, when year by year the holiday crowds grew to a record peak, and the railways felt it was almost a military necessity to accommodate everyone who wished to travel, the strain naturally began to be felt. Much rolling stock, and many sidings and signalboxes shortening sections on mainlines, and controlling crossing loops on branch lines, were only really needed for a handful of peak days. Retired porters and others were temporarily re-employed. Each year, on the day before the busiest Saturday, the yardmaster at Old Oak, outside Paddington insisted: 'It can't be done. It's impossible.' A senior management member soothed him and told him to do his best, and each year he never failed to have a record number of trains marshalled in time to absorb the huge crowds descending on Paddington.

Between the wars, the remodelling of Paddington had largely been planned around the summer Saturday business. Even during the war, many people insisted on a holiday and, at the height of the bombing risk, when the number of trains was strictly rationed, Great Western officials had to plead with Government ones to be allowed to run extras to prevent the possibility of the thousands queuing outside the station being annihilated. In peacetime, from a control coach parked at one of the buffer stops, performance was monitored and strategic decisions taken that normally would have been delegated locally.

Including trains running in several parts and unadvertised extras, the service was never exactly the same two Saturdays running.

Some branch trains were terminated short of the junction with the mainline and given a bus connection and, as an example of congestion, in the 1930s, local trains from Frome and Radstock could be held for up to two hours at the approach to Bristol Temple Meads before being allowed into a platform. Eventually, many minor stations on busy lines were left without calling trains for six or more hours.

Expresses such as *The Atlantic Coast* ran in several advertised parts, all with restaurant cars. On the GWR and Western Region, a special train of restaurant cars, each to work back on different trains the next day, travelled down to Newton Abbot. The crews spent the night dossed down in what later became the David & Charles offices over Newton Abbot's booking hall. The original 1929 tea room failed to take off, but the accommodation then still belonged to the catering side.

Individual seat reservations weren't available on summer Saturdays, but returning passengers had to have a 'regulation' ticket entitling them to use a particular train. When those running at convenient times were already full, that meant an early or late start home – or travelling another day. As will be noted later, regulation booking had been started decades earlier by Blackpool, one of the traditional resorts still busy but where relative fortunes had started to decline as the West Country's rose.

A planning report of around 1950, before the masses went to sun themselves overseas, forecast that tourism in the West Country would flourish as the region attracted 'the more adventurous'. The West Country's increasing popularity was fired by massive advertising campaigns and guide books emphasising large, sandy beaches and a more exotic lifestyle. Especially in the more go-ahead places such as Newquay and Paignton, there was a close relationship between the resorts and the railways. But everywhere the railway was prepared to kick in a contribution, rows of box advertisements in publications such as the *Radio Times* stating: 'It's quicker by train.' Mind you, resorts in other parts of the country, especially the north – Blackpool's budget predictably the highest, uniquely raised by 2d extra on the rates – were no strangers to advertising and fancy guide books for which punters usually had to send a stamp to show their interest was genuine. Until around 1950, almost all northern holidaymakers who could afford to stay away went to the nearest resorts with sandy beaches. Rhyl, Blackpool, Skegness and Scarborough being especially favoured, as were many Welsh and Norfolk resorts by Midlanders.

In England the busiest Saturday was always at the beginning of what became known as the peak fortnight, straddling the old August Bank Holiday weekend. Birmingham and Midland visitors were especially numerous then. That was after many northern towns had their own Wakes Week when everybody seemed to be on holiday apart from railwaymen. Many one-off Wakes Week specials ran to the West Country and other holiday areas

Even in the days of booming goods traffic, apart from the Travelling Post Offices, milk and perishable parcels, passengers were given almost total priority. But the expansion of MotorRail services in the 1950s added to the pressure, many more cars and their passengers being carried especially to the West Country than on other days. Okehampton even had a service to Surbiton, as Inverness did to Perth when the parallel old A9 was notoriously congested. Sleeping car trains multiplied. A Friday night one from Paddington to Penzance was exclusively for Isles of Scilly passengers, which at one time included Harold Wilson, the Prime Minister, heading to his holiday home on St Mary's.

All holiday routes had their pinch points. On the Western it was up Wellington Bank shortly beyond the end of the quadrupled track which carried trains from both the Paddington and Bristol routes through Taunton. Headway up the incline was about six minutes. The Southern's equivalent was longer Honiton Bank.

Yet on most lines saturation point was reached in station platforms. And a hold up at Paignton could result in trains queuing at every available signal back to Dawlish Warren, delaying Cornish-bound services as well as Torbay ones. Trains stopping to change engine crews or take on a banking engine caused their own hold ups. On the Torbay branch, eventually trains were restricted to what one engine could handle, since attaching a banker at Torquay cost too much time. To save shunting movements, coaches might be routed via a branch line in order to change sides of a busy station. Trains being joined or divided, and through carriages (such as at Brent for Kingsbridge) being attached or detached caused more delay with a ripple effect. And remember, rarely was everything on time.

The analysis of delay was fascinating. In steam days, occasional poor locomotive performance, the odd hot axle box and broken signal wire caused occasional trouble. Especially in the Western Region with its hydraulic Warships, Diesels were prone to outright failure. One Saturday evening, just outside Torquay, the steam locomotive which had replaced one failed Diesel ran into the back of another train which had also failed.

This was the stuff of my lead front-page reports in the West Country Sunday and Monday papers, which included details of the number of long-distance passengers (from at least further away than Bristol) arriving at key resorts: perhaps 30,000 between Paignton and Torquay, a jubilant Paignton once overtaking Torquay, and 6,000 at Newquay, at the end of a winding hilly branch, up whose main gradient long trains might require double heading and a banker. Magical sounds echoed through the valley. Once such was the congestion that one train of empty stock had to be sent all the way to Severn Tunnel Junction for siding space.

Summer Saturday traffic reached its peak in 1958, after which my reports became more concerned with road traffic jams: two hours to cover the three miles of the old Exeter bypass was not untypical. As already hinted, the railways never felt they could turn business away, yet that cost them dearly and moreover delayed the spreading of the season.

When parents and especially children suffered long delays in searing conditions, many cars overheating, more visitors took their own action to avoid the worst. Friday and Sunday became busier days. Hotels, boarding houses and even holiday camps were forced to become more flexible, time-honoured compulsory Saturday-to-Saturday bookings at last being abandoned, and the season rapidly started sooner and ended later, helping everyone.

It is sad to reflect that the railways gave so much thought and energy to what proved to have been anti-social. But it was very memorable. I especially recall Exeter St David's, a thronged city in itself at which Great Western and Southern trains often alternated. The Southern up ones, travelling in the same direction as the Western's down ones, all required one or two bankers for lengthy summer Saturday loads up the steep gradient up to Central, so proceedings were punctuated by the ex-LBSC tanks shrilly whistling the long banking code and, returning Light Engine, ready for the next turn. On other days the bankers were more used on the succession of ballast trains from the Southern's own Meldon Quarry.

My examples are inevitably mainly West Country, but much the same was experienced in many holiday areas, so let us run briefly through other resorts, the chief of which was of course Blackpool. It had the most Saturday trains from the greatest number of starting points. Though a thousand Blackpool passengers had been recorded alighting at Poulton on a Saturday in 1841. The branch to Blackpool itself opened in 1846. The resort's rise was slow, and until around 1890 more went to Morecambe. The first town to be electrically lit, and having an early tramway, Blackpool suddenly became the most progressive resort with its famous Tower and ample indoor facilities, outclassing all others and, until the early 1960s, highly dependent on its railways.

The Lancashire & Yorkshire was the first to impose a compulsory reservation system – by train, not individual seat. As trains became full passengers were diverted to others. In 1919, a million passengers were carried this way, 130,000 of them on two August weekends. The press dubbed it 'rationing', but without it the pressure would have risen totally out of control. As it was, there was chaos enough, especially finding stabling room for trains at Blackpool North with its fifteen platforms. Opened in 1903, a New or Morton direct double-track fast route, was opened specially for the Saturday traffic, though it also became used by many excursion trains. It ran from Lytham Junction to serve Blackpool Central which became as important as North.

Nowhere has the decline in the railway's prominence been more marked. Blackpool is no longer the automatic choice of those who used to stay a week, and for day trippers car parking is readily available. Coach competition hurt much earlier than over the longer distances to the South West. Blackpool Central was closed as long ago as at the end of the 1964 Illuminations, the then through trains from London being rerouted to North. The New route was last used on summer Saturdays at the end of the 1965 season, and carried its last excursion trains in 1967. Today's Blackpool South, further from the centre than Central, is a modest terminal and, though it still has its busy moments, even North, rebuilt to a more modest standard on the site of the former excursion platforms outside the original overall roof, has long since ceased to be at the cutting edge of tourism. Regular through trains to London are a thing of the past.

Though under great pressure on peak Saturdays in the 1950s, the busiest of all times at Scarborough was probably over the Bank Holiday in 1939. Between 5.07am and 11.45pm, on that Saturday there were 102 scheduled arrivals and 106 departures at the extremely awkward station to operate. As mentioned in the chapter on excursions, it was impossible to fit in any of those until Sunday.

The Saturday procedure was to detrain passengers at the excursion station, Londesborough Road, and for the train engine to run through the tunnel on the Whitby line, beyond which there were four miles of stabling sidings and locomotive depot. The stock of departing trains had to be propelled into the main station, only one of whose five platforms was full length, and the others differed.

Because the drivers of visiting engines were not familiar with the station, the task was left to the Scarborough crews of shunting engines who backed in briskly, braking at the last moment till the rear coach kissed the buffer. There was not a moment to be wasted between trains, and anything going wrong, such as it being realised that an extra coach had been added making the train too long for its platform, could cause delays whose effect was felt for hours. In this example, the train engine was detached and a shunter hurriedly called for, either to remove the offending vehicle or switch the train to a longer platform.

Scarborough welcomed crowded trains from places as scattered as Glasgow and Leicester as well as London, its mainline also carrying some of the trains via Seamer Junction for the Filey Butlin's camp station just beyond the triangular junction off the mainline. (Others came by the Hull avoiding line also used for the Scarborough–Leicester service, the last of which I used. It was the last advertised passenger train as also on a goods-only short-cut in the Castleford area.)

On summer Saturdays Cleethorpes used to receive several trains from London as well as the industrial north and even the oddity of one from Exmouth, in reality only provided to prevent one terminating and another starting from Birmingham New Street, itself among the pressurised large through stations. Others included Bristol, Leeds, Preston, York, Carlisle and Perth, each with its individual historic-honoured practices and legends.

Trains once reached many more East Coast resorts than today, but Skegness, though now served very indirectly via Sleaforth and Boston, retains a station that still comes thoroughly to life on summer Saturdays. I recall two lengthy trains passing each snaking around a 90 degree turn linking once different routes now abandoned. Since then locomotives have been banned from the deteriorating track, but as this is being written re-laying the entire branch is planned and High Speed Trains may then use it.

The Midland & Great Northern Joint carried many thousands to Cromer and Yarmouth. Melton Constable, where its 'mainline' threw off the Cromer and Norwich branches, attracted almost as many local enthusiasts as the much filmed Somerset & Dorset. Both were among many routes that ordinarily carried a single well-known daily express, but queues of them on summer Saturdays. Thus the one daily *Pines Express* over the S&D and the *Cornishman*, from Birmingham on the Western's North Warwick line via Stratford-upon-Avon, blossomed into a dozen or more on summer Saturdays. Even inland resorts such as Keswick, where the length of the *Lakes Express* was doubled and a second engine added, were pushed to the limit.

Especially in the 1950s, all around Britain through trains and coaches reached many additional places round the coast, including Butlin's camps at places like Ayr and Filey. Bolton Great Moor Street was just one closed station reopened for Wakes Week trains. For a time after 1945, the huge white elephant of Leicester Belgrave Road actually handled decent summer Saturday crowds.

Inland, holiday services took novel cross-country short cuts. Many cross-country links and connecting curves were only used by passengers on summer Saturdays, flocks of 'route and curve bagging' enthusiasts swelling the travelling crowds. Possibly the most surprised of all passengers were those on a through service from Glasgow to Blackpool. Having passed through Preston, a quarter of an hour or so later they went through it again in the reverse direction – just one of many measures taken to prevent trains occupying valuable platform space.

Scotland was always different, schools breaking up earlier and Glasgow Fair soon following, with one-off through working to unlikely places such as Banff. I've often mentioned that on summer Saturdays in the 1950s, two trains originated in Nairn, both for Edinburgh, via the long-abandoned route across the wild Dava between Forres and Aviemore. Carrying mainly Scots, one of them terminated at Waverley, the other at Princess Street.

When things were busy, they also tended to be friendlier. There was certainly no time for staff to sit around complaining. Signalmen at crossing loops on single-line branches to the resorts no longer exercised a degree of personal choice or selfishness over where late trains crossed but did their utmost to save the odd minute. In my experience it was only on the former Cambrian line to Pwllheli, where most staff spoke Welsh, that delays were greater than they need have been. Summer Saturday timekeeping on it was awful. Crossing loops with only one platform did not help.

Thus, returning to the West Country, remarkably perhaps in view of the historic rivalry, Western and Southern men seemed on good terms at Exeter St David's when things went wrong, as when one of the series of *Atlantic Coast Expresses* just failed to clear the points at its rear. A whole succession of steps had to be taken rapidly to arrange for it to pull forward a yard. Another memory is of the driver of a King on a train signalled to run non-stop through the middle platformless road, stopping opposite me on the down platform's up end when he spotted that I had a copy of the working timetable.

'You know, I think I'm meant to stop here, check could you.' When I confirmed he should, his fireman giggling, he added:

'Young man, run along to Control as quickly as you can.'

RAILWAY OCCASIONS

FROM THE FAMOUS Rainhill Trials to pick the best locomotive for the Liverpool & Manchester Railway spectacularly won by Stephenson's *Rocket*, railways have excelled at getting themselves in the news. What I call Railway Occasions have been varied and still continue giving much pleasure as well as grabbing the headlines.

Spring, when improvements in the summer timetable were announced (now to conform with EU it is December) was for generations a notable publicity point. Then, staff and enthusiasts, sometimes the press, kept a particular eye on the first day's performance of the new service. Did accelerated trains run to time? Did revised connections work smoothly? What were loadings like, as when a new non-stop to Exmouth was followed three minutes later by an all-station service? Were stationmaster's forebodings about problems proved right or wrong? In the days that a late Saturday evening train still ran on many lines, did the further cut-back in how far the train went, such as on the Waverley route from Edinburgh toward Carlisle, and the line south from Aberystwyth, mean that the number of passengers at the starting point had so reduced to make total withdrawal inevitable?

Each summer Saturday, as described in chapter X, was a Railway Occasion, almost a sporting one. Each season's first was watched with special care. Had lessons been learnt from the previous summer? Could an extra train be sandwiched in without making following ones later? Was it really necessary further to prevent trains calling at intermediate stations, and even stop some branch ones from reaching the mainline at all?

At the other extreme, advance details of winter Sunday services disturbed many stationmasters. Traffic was undoubtedly thin on winter Sunday mornings, but wasn't the railway meant to be a public service? Conversely, arrangements for getting people back to London and other big cities on Sunday evenings were often woefully inadequate, and for years one looked in vain for improvements. When a district manager told me that too many people travelled on the last train, so to get a seat his daughter returned on the second last, two hours earlier, the response to my suggestion that there should be two last trains, accelerated by serving different secondary stations, was: 'Why hasn't anyone thought of that?'

It's fun seeing changing attitudes reflected in old timetables, for example how slow the railways were to realise that increasingly businessmen were prepared to spend a long day on the go in preference to having to travel overnight. Once the West Coast mainline was at its most congested in the small hours with sleepers and carriages with passengers sitting bolt upright, mail and newspaper trains and processions of goods ones.

Accelerations were often pioneered by test runs, themselves Railway Occasions. Passengers normally were, and on special runs still are, confined to civic dignitaries, officials, and railway and local journalists, vying with each other to make the most of the experience.

Speed tests are exciting. With almost a Mafia-like atmosphere, familiar faces and voices are brought together, experiences and views swapped before things get under way. As departure time approaches, those timing runs in detail take a facing window seat with stop-watch and notebook – and an earnestness which says 'Don't disturb'. When a railway journalist is allowed on the footplate, the precise manner in which the controls are handled is included in the report, though driving techniques matter much less today than when steam reigned.

All participants, and indeed onlookers, hope for the best. Starting time will have been arranged to reduce the likelihood of delay but, when the unpredictable happens, and everyone is anxious as a supposedly non-stop trial is brought to a standstill. There is always some allowance for delay, and usually things work out. On the mainline to the West Country, I recall my secretary waving at me as arranged from the office beside the track at Newton Abbot (193 miles from Paddington) exactly two hours after departure. It was then an all time record. On the return from Plymouth by the long way round, ignoring a generous intended lay-over at Bristol, we took just 3 hours and 16 minutes. With more powerful engines, that paved the way for some regular trains going by the direct route from Paddington to Plymouth in 3½ hours with three stops, half an hour less than steam's non-stop fastest.

That palls into insignificance compared with the 126mph reached by the LNER's A4 *Mallard* for a few seconds on a test run in 1938, which has remained the world's fastest official speed record for steam. Today speed is limited by engineers controlling the track, but then it was up to the driver. The A4s undoubtedly paved the way for the East Coast's speeding up, some of today's trains regularly achieving higher point-to-point long-distance speeds than reached on at least one of Europe's new dedicated high-speed lines. The preserved A4s are allowed to run on mainline specials at 80mph, far faster than other types. Exciting indeed were the journalists' reports of that 1938 run. Some by expert railway commentators are still read.

Locomotive trials, machines of one railway running on routes of others, have also been great Railway Occasions. Many expected that those just after nationalisation would be useful in determining what further building of the locomotives of the four Grouping

Era companies might take place. In the event, a whole new series of standard classes were built. But there was still a great feeling of rivalry involving enthusiasts as well as staff. I felt proud that the Great Western's 4-6-0s performed well against the other three's 4-6-2 Pacifics.

My only personal memory is a run to Teignmouth on the 1.30pm from Paddington in 1948. For some reason our seats were at the back of the lengthy train. Not hearing the whistle, we first realised there was a 'foreigner' at the sharp end on seeing unaccustomed crowds line embankments and bridges and their approaches. Then someone said it was *Seagull*, another A4. So we moved forward and heard the melodious chime rather than the Great Western's shrill whistle. Performance was excellent, though starting the heavy load wasn't as sure-footed as the GWR's.

Major anniversaries with great exhibitions, and the introduction of a new train or rolling stock also brought, and still occasionally do bring, the railway press together. It isn't hard to make a special publicity-orientated Railway Occasion. Locomotive-naming still attract crowds, the guests usually first having enjoyed a celebratory meal. On the move, restaurant cars with luxury food and wine used to be attached to special trains. Ordinary press conferences aren't in the same league though, even for them, railways have traditionally looked after reporters better than most industries or official organisations.

Meals also played – and still can – a vital part in days out on inspection saloons, controllable from the front end when propelled. It has to be said that some trips made by railwaymen themselves, such as on a branch line about to be closed, or even just after closure, were more for their pleasure than usefulness – especially when closure followed years of deliberately running things down.

For varying reasons, I was occasionally allowed to choose an itinerary, with memorable moments. When I directed the Lake District Transport Enquiry, we parked in a siding at Keswick, and I asked why the engine had moved away. The answer epitomised the attention to detail. 'So you can enjoy your lunch in peace, sir.' The on-board chef, working in a small kitchen in the inspection saloon's centre, enquired how one liked one's meat. We were spoiled.

When my editor was also invited on a couple of circular trips in Devon and Cornwall, I mentioned he was a cricket enthusiast. So at every station the stationmaster stood to attention waiting to greet us with the latest score. Many of those stations have long since closed, the remainder no longer have a stationmaster, and today one could get the latest score on the mobile.

Well after nationalisation, railways continued to advertise excursions, cheap fares and new services in virtually every newspaper in the land. With the help of special occasions railways are still adept at being in the news for good news and bad for free.

Open days at depots are popular, while I recall great run-pasts of engines ancient and modern celebrating the 150th anniversary of the pioneer Stockton & Darlington at Shildon and five years later of the Liverpool & Manchester. When an inspection saloon passes it is still noticed – as of course is the breakdown train on the way to an accident, usually a simple derailment not on a track used by passengers. The Royal Train is another attention drawer. The older among us recall with special fondness the funeral train of King George VI,

and the photograph of track workers just outside Paddington station paying their respects.

Enthusiasts' specials have long been Railway Occasions – especially those running to the extremities of the system and on branch lines including those that have never normally had a passenger service. For instance, in strings of guard's vans, Plymouth's Railway Circle explored Cornwall's extensive china-clay lines. We gave advice on shunting when things became stale-mated. I also enjoyed a journalist's permission to travel on the clay lines, including through Cornwall's longest railway tunnel where, with the fumes of a banker, one could hardly breathe. After one serious smoke-filled incident, banking was stopped. Later, when the clay industry bought the line and converted it to a road, I did a broadcast through the tunnel on a lorry. Not nearly as romantic.

Often railway societies organised a final post-public closure on a branch, which naturally attracted much attention. Today's specials for enthusiasts tend to travel further, even over a long weekend from Penzance to Wick. And since steam was allowed back onto the national system, it has created much public as well as enthusiast interest. A few services are now semi-regular, but it is the one-off occasions that hit the news and bring out the crowds. English enthusiasts are enthralled by Scotland's long scenic routes and a series of specials using the locomotive of that season's choice for the summer regulars from Fort William to Mallaig have become notable Railway Occasions. Different itineraries are used before the locomotive finally returns south.

The special thing missing today is the spare rolling stock that could be called upon for excursion trains: see chapter on Excursions. But then, as said in the chapter on Railways for Pleasure, today's heritage railways organise nearly a thousand special events a year. As long as there are trains, Railway Occasions will flourish, for they lend themselves well to performing the unusual with panache. Even closures (or 'railway funerals', see the last chapter) have been sensational. And to leave in style, today you can arrange for your coffin to travel on a train on a heritage line as part of your own funeral.

THE NATURAL HISTORY
OF THE RAILWAY

'LEAVES ON THE line' is as famous a reason for trains being late in autumn as the 'Wrong kind of snow' in winter. It wasn't always so, for in steam days embankments and cuttings were scythed and burnt each summer, a labour-intensive activity which prevented both lineside fires and the spread of other vegetation. It maintained the excellence of the grass and especially its spring flowers. That the quality of the underlying soil was often poor led to the colonisation of many rarer species.

Many of us must first have become aware of the vast richness of Britain's flora from the comfort of a railway carriage, perhaps a local train plodding slowly uphill, or of an express whose progress had been impeded by signal delay or speed restriction. Even when speed prevented identification of single plants, the colour of massed bluebells, or primroses, poppies, thistle-like knapweeds, yellow-flowered golden rod and oxy-eye daisies was unmistakeable, as were the foamy-grey seed hairs of old man's beard in autumn. Regional variations of course abounded, cowslips in Sussex and Hampshire and harebells in Scotland especially coming to mind.

The railway provided a remarkably stable habitat. In steam days it couldn't be too overgrown for safety's sake, and so in good weather was usually sunny for at least part of the day. The engineers insisted it was well drained, as they still do. And it was remarkably undisturbed. Even on the busiest of lines there were usually fewer trains than there was cars on most country lanes. Pedestrians were rare. Many years passed between major engineering upheavals, the greatest disturbances being caused by the annual passage of the weedkilling train, but spraying has always been well controlled, affecting only a narrow strip beyond the ballast.

Each embankment had and still has its own mini environment, with a notable difference between the vegetation of south and north-facing ones. The damp, cool slopes of the north-facing were often rich in mosses and liverworts. The appearance of the velvety mosses was particularly familiar. The strangely-named liverworts, similar to mosses but without distinct stems and leaves, consist of fronds that lie flat on the ground. They got their names because the fronds of some species resemble the lobes of the liver.

The south-facing banks, well-lit and drained, supported a large proportion of the 1300 or so species of British wildflowers. Some may still be seen growing within a few feet of the rails, though traditionally their range increased slightly further away.

Though the summer scything and controlled burning of vegetation on embankments in steam days was generally beneficial, it encouraged bracken and the ubiquitous rose-bay willow herb to such an extent that they tended to take over in places – and still do. In America the willow herb is called fireweed, not for its brilliant flower-spikes but for its colonisation of areas where there have been fires. Its seeds are tolerant of heated soil and so are able to establish a hold before other plants. Each produces around 80,000 seeds. Each seed has a long plume of about seventy silk hairs which act like a parachute and waft it along on the summer breezes or in the slipstream of a passing vehicle. By the end of July there was scarcely a railway line that did not have its mass of purple flowers and, though it is not quite so common now, in late August and September clouds of seeds can still be drifting in the air. Once a seed has settled in the right sort of soil, it quickly sends out runners a short distance below the surface. Roots can spread three feet in a season, sending up new shoots all the time.

Altogether the traditional railway embankment used to contain one of the richest and most varied collections of flowers of any habitat. Railways probably owned as many rare species as the National Trust.

1968 was the date when cutting and burning of grass was finally abandoned. Since then woodland has advanced more rapidly on railway land, along open lines as well as closed, than in any other British environment. Narrow strips of linear woodland as well as embankments and cuttings tell of abandoned routes. Nature abhors a vacuum. Once lines have been closed and the rails removed, the process is set in motion. Much the same thing applies to land once occupied by sidings and depots along lines still open.

Coarse grasses, docks, nettles, thistles and brambles move in, larger slow-growing shrubs such as elder and hawthorn steadily taking over, frequently competing with brambles for light. The hawthorn is especially prevalent on the Midlands plain. Broom has conquered embankments of many closed lines in Suffolk, gorse in Pembrokeshire, bracken and wild raspberry in Scotland, to quote some regional variations. Grassland flowers steadily disappear, though bluebells struggle on and, should the larger vegetation be cut back, spring into a glorious display next season.

Well over 6,000 miles of railway route have now been abandoned in Britain and, though housing, industrial development and road schemes have swept many into oblivion, deep in the country (especially in hilly country and beside rivers) thousands of miles will remain undisturbed for generations to come. Only a few routes have become dedicated footpaths or cycleways. In other cases the passage of human beings will keep open a track through an increasingly dense woodland; others, in due time, will become native forest, the oak no doubt eventually becoming dominant in many western areas, depriving most other vegetation of adequate light. But the process will not be completed for centuries to come. Oak and beech are normally confined to cuttings, but the quick-growing ash will eventually tower over uncut scrub in many environments.

For many years evidence of that greatest of enthusiasm, gardening, of railwaymen of bygone days will still be found. Mint and rhubarb come up each year where signalmen and platelayers once tended their plots; blackberries and raspberries have crossed the boundaries into what used to be the plots of rival railwaymen's gardens; even where the platform edges have disappeared, the roses continue to flower, albeit in a straggly way, and once neat lonicera hedges assume forest proportions.

That trees are advancing more rapidly on railway land, open and closed, than elsewhere is all too obvious to those of us with long memories, for many views we once enjoyed have been obliterated. There are two routes, at opposite ends of the country, where personally I've felt the greatest impact. One is between Charing Cross and Folkestone. As a boy on the way to Hythe for holidays with Mum's family, I gazed in awe at views of an unfamiliar landscape as our steam engine roared down favourable gradients and struggled up the climbs on the undulating route across the Downs. Once I recall the engine having to pause outside a tunnel to build up steam pressure to continue. Oast houses passed in succession. Today you will spot few, even those converted into stylish houses, for much of the way it is trees and more trees. You won't now see any hop fields either.

The other route is the first part of the Mallaig extension of the West Highland line from Fort William beside Loch Eil. This is where one's excitement used to increase, but in recent years only occasional glimpses could be caught between the trees. Since this is a tourist line, a subsidised plan has been announced to open up the view again. That is unlikely to happen generally, though the heritage lines, such as the Isle of Wight Steam Railway, are well aware of the need to protect views. Most of the steam railways, and the reintroduction of occasional steam on the Fort William-Mallaig line, happened after trees had become well established, being at less of a risk of catching fire from a spark than the traditional grassland verges they replaced or the first stages of coarse growth leading to woodland.

Things are never static. Train speeds increase, relaying methods are revolutionised, weedkilling procedures become more sophisticated as does the equipment for removing slimy layers of compressed autumn leaves from the rails. Though all four of the pre-nationalised railways had their weedkilling trains, great advances have been made since. Public attitudes have also been sharpened. There has been an ongoing dialogue between railwaymen and conservationists.

The LNER long had an unwelcome policy of replacing hedges with concrete posts and chains, but earlier several companies gave their staff detailed instructions on how to encourage growth to make stronger hedges. And once trees have become established, and in many cases coppiced, there are objections to them being hacked about with unsightly flailing done by sharp blades projecting from a special carriage.

There was an especial outcry at the extent of trees and coppice clearance for the St Pancras-Bedford electrification in the late 1970s. Part of it was done at the insistence of the railway inspectorate for safety, and the rest for economy, one major clearance being cheaper than two lesser ones. The pendulum then swung in the tree preservation's direction until the Seer Green accident happened on the former Great Central line out of Marylebone. Though the signalling system should have avoided it, a second train ran into the back of the first – halted by trees bowed down by the weight of snow. So the clearance lobby regained power and further electrification projects saw more destruction of trees and especially of coppice. The special danger of limbs falling off trees on the unstable London clays has always had to be kept in mind.

In British Rail days a director for the environment liaised with the Nature Conservancy Council and other bodies. The *Biological Survey of British Rail Property* of 1980 by the Institute of Terrestrial Ecology of the Nature Environment Research Council listed many dozens of sites, mainly grassland, where conservation was considered especially valuable. For example, many of the sites, including nine between King's Cross and Grantham, were previously managed by the annual cutting and burning, and scrub were then controlled with the involvement of the Nature Conservancy Council, saving refuges of our natural grasslands, with mixtures of grasses and herbaceous plants dependent on the local conditions and soil, the more rare examples again often being found on exposed areas of poorer soils.

Says the introduction to the *Biological Survey:* 'The excavated slopes tend to have a nutrient poor mineral soil which supports locally and regionally characteristic plants, and inhibits competition from false oat, even where previously burnt'. It goes on to stress that priority should be given to the maintenance of cuttings. 'Scything and occasional burning of grassland will prevent the development of scrub, whilst encouraging diversity. Burning, however, should only be carried out over limited areas of verge and not at all during the bird nesting season'.

Privatisation's change to Railtrack broke continuity, especially with its policy of 'sweating its assets', for example saving money even by failing to remove sizeable plants cracking the stonework of Brunel's splendid approach from London into Bath. More recently, under National Rail, attitudes have become more mature, though predictably my enquiries were unanswered. Though many views will remain obstructed over thousands of miles of line, if the train isn't going too fast, it is still eminently well worth looking sharp down out of the window to see what plant life survives.

If one had to nominate the 'railway flower', it might be the small (or lesser) toadflax, only 3-9 inches high, growing profusely in the ballast of railway tracks that are not frequently sprayed (such as little-used and abandoned sidings). It has spread along railways to all parts of the British Isles except northern Scotland, displaying its little snapdragon-like flowers from June to September; like chickweed, it is an annual with tiny white flowers growing in clusters between April and September. Then there is sticky groundsel with its yellow blossoms, after which come the seeds each with their own parachute of fine white hairs, and the rarer strapwort growing low over the ground and producing clusters of red-tipped white flowers in June to August.

Aquilegia or blue columbine and primroses can flourish within feet of rapidly passing tons of metal. The lovely blue meadow cranesbill, too, has no happier environment. The tall, brilliant yellow evening primrose quickly takes hold if the ground has been disturbed by engineering works and, if the embankment drops to a stream or ditch, you can not only look down on, but listen to the Himalayan balsam when its seed pods explode at the end of summer. A handsome, tall, pink flower, it has expanded rapidly in recent times.

Trains often help in the distribution of species, sometimes through spreading seeds in their slipstreams, others by physically carrying seeds and spores. Thus, in steam days, scarce ferns used to grow and luxuriate from the moist brickwork near stations and tunnels, often hundreds of miles out of their usual range. Supposedly typical seaside plants may still be seen growing readily in the shingle-like ballast, if not in tracks that have been sprayed, on the ballast thrown just clear at renewal time, or in rusting sidings.

The yellow biting stonecrop or wall pepper is a creeping plant often found in goods sidings but is more at home colouring rocks, cliffs and walls with patches of bright yellow during the summer. It has succulent leaves which store water, enabling it to survive weeks of summer drought. Another example is the yellow-flowered wild wallflower, usually found on cliffs and in quarries but quite capable of surviving on railway tracks. And in the same way that Roman soldiers carried Mediterranean species along our first road system, around goods yards where imported fleeces used to be unloaded, you can find weeds of Australia and South American origin.

One of the most curious stories is that of the yellow daisy-like Oxford ragwort. It was introduced from Sicily to Britain in 1699 in the Oxford Botanic Gardens. A century later it broke out from the gardens and spread along the Oxford walls. Almost another century later it reached the Great Western Railway, and then spread rapidly along the system, taking to the ballast and clinker ash as though it were around its native Mount Etna. Eventually the GWR passed it on to other railways, the seeds with their little parachutes no doubt literally being carried by trains as well as in their slipstreams. It is now common over much of Britain, commoner here than anywhere else in the world.

I especially love those little pockets of land rendered useless to agriculture, perhaps where the railway temporarily abandons running alongside a river or stream. But then most people will only ever see teasels from a train. It naturally helps if you know where to look.

Broadening our perspective, railwaymen have always been keen observers of animal and bird life. Most naturalists would be envious of the number of occasions train drivers see foxes and, in parts of Scotland, deer. Passengers are more likely to catch glimpses of rabbits and the larger, long-eared hares, oblivious of noise and danger from trains as they indulge in their March ritual running around in circles in the fields. Rabbits abound on railway embankments, especially when the vegetation is not cut. Generations of children have spotted rabbits at play while waiting to see an evening train pass; generations of railwaymen have supplemented their diet with rabbits they have caught. Much of animal life on railway property is secret in the undergrowth, preying birds being our clue to the often dense populations of voles, shrews and mice. Rats have always been carefully controlled near depots, but what few people see, and are much harder to control, are foxes using railways secretly to penetrate urban areas.

Birds are much more evident, trains making perfect 'hides'. Herons and other estuary birds thus take far less notice of an express train with hundreds of people on board than the passage of a single walker along the shore. Many birds feel safer on a railway track, on a motorway or near an airport, than in ordinary fields, and owls, buzzards and kestrels are among those making good use of railway furniture.

The replacement of most telegraph poles by underground systems and the felling of many farmland trees and hedges have placed a premium on perches, and a signal may be regularly used between forays by the day-hunting kestrel, though you are more likely to spot the bird hovering in the air with its tail fanned out and wings flapping gently as it surveys the ground for mice and voles to snatch.

A number of 'ground' birds are readily identified from a train. In Scotland there is the red grouse living in the heather-clad moorlands, beating low over the ground with a whirring flight when disturbed. Pheasants are often to be seen close to the train in East Anglia and Southern England – but are more seriously studied by railwaymen than passengers. The ganger has always been the most difficult poacher for the gamekeeper with no direct authority over the narrow strip of railway land passing through an estate. Partridges often nest in the undergrowth on embankments, parents and young taking no notice of the trains, but at risk when grass is cut or burnt. Many an instruction has gone out from headquarters requesting staff to take care not to destroy nests. The railway has always been part of the countryside it serves, seasonal instructions also include taking care to avoid running down a hunt in full flight, though until fox hunting was banned accidents still occasionally happened.

The railway habitat is perhaps particularly valuable for butterflies, the most denuded of our types of wildlife through the rationalisation of farm boundaries and increasing use of insecticides. Honeybees and bumblebees and all kinds of flies and insects abound, too, the railway embankment literally buzzing more loudly than adjoining farmland, reminding us what we have lost in the countryside through factory farming.

Tunnels and bridges have their own story. Ferns (usually at the north end) of bridges and tunnels, were 'watered' by the steam of passing locomotives. Bats quickly colonise disused tunnels and often co-exist uneasily with trains in those still open. They were known to be within the 'tunnel' or tube of Stephenson's famous bridge over the Menai Straits, connecting Anglesea to the mainland, and it was because a couple of young wildlife enthusiasts went into the darkness in search of them that Irish boat trains were unable to reach Holyhead for a considerable period: the lads accidentally set fire to the bitumen lining the tube, and the tube itself buckled. It was a spectacular fire, presumably destroying the bats.

Every fire, every piece of engineering work, takes its toll of some form of wildlife and makes it easier for another to gain a foothold or increase its strength. Yet even the modern railway provides a relatively safe home for countless species, and closed branch lines and other pieces of land not used by man form our most valuable unofficial nature reserve. A few sections of closed line are in fact official reserves, the best known being Haskayne Cutting in Lancashire, about two miles of the former Southport & Cheshire Lines Extension route between Warrington and Southport. Part of it is in a narrow cutting, part more open, where Altcar & Hillhouse station once stood, where passengers by rail motor from Southport Chapel Street could change to a train from Southport Lord Street bound for Warrington and Manchester. The last trains ran in 1952, and many years passed before the Lancashire Trust for Nature Conservation moved in. Near Ormskirk, Haskayne Cutting is now run by the Wildlife Trust for Lancashire, Manchester & North Merseyside and contains a surprising diversity of habitats: 172 vascular plants and 60 species of birds (of which 37 are thought to breed on the site) and 14 species of butterfly have been recorded.

Finally back to flowers for a last mention, a special prize are the magenta pink, yellow-centred and all-yellow succulent mesembryanthemums that, when the weather has been favourable, bloom on the cliffs overlooking the Sea Wall between Dawlish and Teignmouth. After a late heavy frost they almost disappear, but sure enough they come back to life and spread anew, the pink ones more readily, and command a great audience from trains as well as those walking along the Sea Wall. Native to South Africa, they escaped gardens in mild South Devon and are strictly not wild.

Then, as with the human population, it is increasingly difficult to know who and what is 'native'. Were he to return, the Duke of Wellington might be impressed by all the monuments to him but would be horrified at how the railways muddled things up.

RAILWAYS FOR PLEASURE

PASSENGERS ARRIVE EARLY and are in no hurry to leave at journey's end. They smile. So do the staff. Relaxed, they cheerfully talk to each other. Stations are well equipped if somewhat old fashioned. On the train, passengers watch the passing scenery and point things out to each other through large windows. Hardly anyone has their face buried in a book or is playing a computer game. Strikes are unknown. For most staff, annual pay rises are a non-event since they don't get paid anyway. There's no government subsidy, yet the books balance happily.

Welcome to the world of railways for pleasure, which mainly take the form of what have become known as heritage lines, though many people also take journeys for pleasure on steam and other specials including the two British Orient Express trains whose staff are in regular employment.

Why are so many people involved in railways for pleasure? Stepping back in time to celebrate our yesterdays in style first comes to mind. Nostalgia for steam, for the machine that first carried man faster than an animal and was universal in much of Britain well into the 1950s, is obviously strong. Boys of all ages worship yesteryear's steam engines, and now the first brand-new modern one is busily at work on mainline charters.

Today's drivers on the heritage lines include what, because of the passage of time, is inevitably a declining number of former professional engine men. Most are amateurs who long harboured a desire to get their hands on a regulator. And many railways add to their income by teaching other enthusiasts how to drive a locomotive, a challenge that makes a wonderful Christmas present.

But, as some lines dependent on diesels demonstrate, there's more to it than steam. As well as the full-blown railways proper, many zoos and seaside resorts sport mini-railways, some with passengers sitting astride in single file. Old and young seem equally happy to ride on flanged wheels even on the mini-permanent way.

On heritage lines, the track and general infrastructure is certainly an important ingredient. To many, just restoring a route, using well-renovated old buildings, and allowing passengers again to enjoy once-familiar views of the countryside from seats well aligned with windows, is itself a worthy aim. Each volunteer and passenger no doubt has their interest or obsession made up of a slightly different mix.

Comradeship is also important for those who operate, maintain and support the heritage lines. Most lines have members (the larger ones thousands of them) of an organisation separated from that which physically owns and runs the hardware. Quarterly issues of their magazines are eagerly read. Behind it all there is an almost religious fervour, and great harmony. Rank matters little. People from every walk of life from Lords to the most humble manual workers and their wives work with a common purpose and a sparkle in their eyes.

Generally, no sport, hobby or whatever you call it is more at home with itself. And during the season, probably only fishing has more active adherents than the voluntary railway movement, though some of the larger lines do employ a nucleus of salaried staff.

We sometimes need to remind ourselves that the most significant changes in Britain's appearance and way of life in the last two centuries have been caused by three major waves that left little of the country untouched. The first was industrialisation. The second suburbanisation. The third leisure.

The railways played the leading role in the first two. The more recent emphasis on leisure is partly due to the decline of our industrial base, partly to the inpouring of overseas visitors, while cars and coaches have substantially reduced the railway's contribution. However, it is still considerable. The railways echo what has happened in so much of the rest of the economy.

Today leisure is a thing apart. Take fine dining on the move. Once, as explored in chapter X, at least for the top slice of society, it was part and parcel of the everyday travel experience. Now to enjoy a fine lunch or dinner in spacious surroundings you have to turn to a special service that is part of our burgeoning leisure business. Many routes closed because of mounting losses have been revived by leisure.

It comes as a surprise to learn that if all the heritage lines were to be put in a continuous line, it would stretch from King's Cross to Blair Atholl in the foothills of the Cairngorms. Extensions now planned would extend the route to Dingwall, north of Inverness. At the time of writing, around fifty years since the first was reopened, collectively the preserved or voluntary railways make up a system greater than London's Underground.

Preserved railways are big business. Including a few Irish ones, their current 500 or so miles serve 356 stations. They earn over £70 million carrying over 6 million passengers yearly. Even on existing lines the number is still growing. Writing in *Railwatch* serving the interests of keen rail users, Chris Austin calculates that they employ around 1,700 people backed by armies of volunteers making a substantial contribution to the economy. The amateur railwaymen themselves spend money fulfilling their hobby or obsession. The longest preserved standard-gauge line, the West Somerset, estimates that for every pound spent by travellers on fares, an additional £1.90 is poured into the local economy.

This hasn't been achieved without sacrifice and heartache. When it was called British Railways, steam was once prohibited on the national system because it was seen as 'psychologically disturbing to the staff'. Every obstacle was placed in the way of people seen as enthusiasts. When one of the less-foresighted general managers met me as journalist and broadcaster, his opening comment was: 'Thomas, I do hope you are not an enthusiast.' Early sale agreements were hedged with over-protective clauses for BR. Thus, when the narrow-gauge line from Aberystwyth to Devil's Bridge, by then long a purely seasonal

tourist affair, was sold, BR retained optic cable rights along the route together with half of any other development rights.

Especially when volunteers demonstrated their professional skills, attitudes steadily changed, and eventually British Rail, as it had become, was not adverse to earning a bob or two from allowing steam specials on selected routes, though again with inflexible conditions – which local staff sometimes delighted in setting aside in the interests of common sense and their own railway interest. One of the more enlightened policies of today's National Rail is to donate redundant track and even an occasional bridge to heritage lines.

At one time, the link between the national system and what was to become a heritage line was automatically severed, and everything done to prevent restoration. Thus, though there was no practical reason why the West Somerset Railway might not have become even longer with its own independent access to its own bay platform and run-round at Taunton, signal posts were speedily erected in the old track bed. The official policy was one of opposition because the National Union of

Railwaymen didn't like it. They needed to protect the interest of the bus drivers on the route who were members because until 1930 the buses had been railway owned.

For years before the sparse clay traffic ceased, it would have been perfectly feasible for the trains from Swanage, now operated by well-trained volunteers, to have shared the rails as they had done in BR's ownership. Impossible. Now that the whole route has been abandoned by the national system, a link has been cautiously allowed, a Virgin Cross Country train being given a great welcome at Swanage.

Far greater crowds, voting with their feet, gathered to see the first train cross the level crossing between the national system and the long isolated North Norfolk Railway at Sheringham. Signalling costs had been cited as the reason why the link had to be broken and couldn't be restored. With a touch of common sense, the link has been restored *unsignalled*. Ad hoc arrangements with police protection for the few occasions on which a special will run each year is a far cheaper option and yet the through trains will significantly help an area in need of a boost.

As it happens, I have a Patron's role on both the South Devon Railway running alongside the freshwater Dart, and the Strathspey at the other end of the country. Both are among the mere eighteen heritage railways that so far have an operational link with the national system, but both were fraught with initial difficulty and what can only be called childish behaviour on the part of the national system. For example, when the Strathspey was belatedly allowed to use one side of an island platform at Aviemore, an expensive fence with a narrow gateway was erected the platform's length to demonstrate what was whose.

Both the South Devon and Speyside had ambitions to grow. The South Devon wanted to get back to its original terminus at Ashburton. Opposition came from the Devon County Council which had opposed earlier closure and now wanted the land for the widened A38 though, if sensibly planned, there was no reason why both couldn't have been accommodated.

Yesterday (as I write this), I was among invited guests on a special inspection saloon that ran on a short piece of route not used since 1966. The event launched an appeal for funds to take trains back into Grantown-on-Spey on an extended Strathspey Railway. It will cost £5 million for three miles, over £1 million just for an underpass to cross the A95 trunk road between Aviemore and Grantown. There's great confidence that it will be achieved.

It is by this route, the Highland Railway's original one, that in the 1950s I first travelled through Nairn, where I've lived for the last twenty years. Once in Grantown I even shared a taxi from the former Great North of Scotland's station to that of the Highland. New housing unfortunately prevents the replacement line reaching the town centre. British Railways were in a reckless hurry to prevent routes ever being reopened, and Parliament took no interest. In Ireland track beds were better preserved, helping with reopenings there. That such ambitious expensive schemes can now be undertaken shows how the voluntary railway movement has come of age. A few years ago the Severn Valley Railway succeeded in rapidly raising a five-figure sum to repair extensive flood damage

The most ambitious of all schemes has been the rebuilding of the Welsh Highland Railway. Including a section of the former standard-gauge line out of Caernarfon, it will provide a 40-mile narrow-gauge route all the way from Caernarfon to Blaenau Ffestiniog.

Closed in the 1930s, the Welsh Highland long ago caught the fancy of enthusiasts studying details and pictures in old books, drooling especially over Charles E Lee's *Narrow-Gauge Railways in North Wales*, published in 1945. Then the Ffestiniog itself was in its last death throes. Seeing that reopened, especially as part was buried under a reservoir, necessitating a diversion through a new tunnel, has been miracle enough. It is a glorious line with fine scenery beautifully engineered including a long section on a narrow shelf carved in the hillside. The continuous downhill gradient was for slate trains run by gravity. On the 1ft 11¾ins gauge, you can enjoy refreshments in a fabulous observation car.

The rebuilding of the Welsh Highland has been fraught with problems. At first the Snowdonia National Park was dead against it, but then saw that it could be a marvellous means of carrying people on a thin strip of land blending into the landscape into the heart and through Snowdonia, re-using a series of short tunnels pierced through a hillside which remained a point of interest over the three score and ten trainless years. The passengers now going through them cause far less disturbance than car travellers needing to park en route. I wrote about its progress, and seeing a further section of track added by volunteers, in *Journey Through Britain*.

There were many obstacles: raising millions of pounds, uneasy relations with the group claiming to be the original Welsh Highland, and a level-crossing over a main road into Porthmadog. No sooner had track been laid over the crossing than the police filled in the gap where the wheels of trains run saying it was dangerous to cyclists.

Not least among the worries is the need to attract many new and different passengers. Most people who enjoy a train journey for pleasure have only limited time. Many will surely choose a trip on either the Welsh Highland or Ffestiniog. Very careful marketing will be needed. For me the real joy will be a circular trip using BR via Llandudno Junction and a short section by road between Bangor and Caernafon – but that will be an all-day job. Even the one-way journey from Caernarfon to Blaenau Ffestiniog will take four hours, usually with a change of train at Porthmadog.

As a group, most offering a short though memorable journey, the Little Trains of Wales have certainly boosted the area's economy. They include the Talyllyn from Towyn, always a friendly line and, like the Ffestiniog and several others, built for the slate trade. As vividly

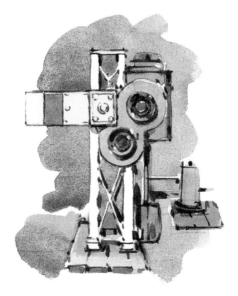

described in L T C Rolt's *Railway Adventure*, the Talyllyn was the world's first railway to be rescued by volunteers... as the Bluebell Railway in Sussex was the first piece of ex-BR to spring back to life.

Popular Santa specials aiding cash flow when otherwise things would be dormant, and Thomas days or weekends (with heavy charges by the money-making franchise holder which the gentle parson author of the Thomas books would have hated) are among nearly a thousand special events a year held by the heritage railways.

Yet sometimes, especially early and late in the season, it is possible to experience riverside, lakeside or to climb through the hills almost in isolation as one could in ordinary railway days. My only problem is that, in the same way that reopened canals have strings of boats moored along them, even at wayside stations such as Staverton, on my own joyous South Devon Railway, there are new sidings and parked rolling stock. There is always a danger of the leisure industry spoiling itself.

Yet the busiest line of all, the North Yorkshire Moors, though long trains are crowded, there is still a splendid atmosphere among both staff (100 paid and many volunteers) and passengers. Once with a rope-worked incline, it is a route of tough gradients – and splendid scenery. Not only do steam trains from Pickering work through on the national rail to Whitby at the end of the Esk Valley line, but at busy times others link Whitby with Battersby. Serving a wide range of interests, the North Yorkshire Moors Railway is a serious as well as pleasure-giving business and has done much for the local economy.

FLOODS AND STORMS

IF YOU KNOW your railway geography and have a reasonably good memory, you can cast your eye around a map and recall the flooding and storms that have affected the system over the years. Few British or Irish mainlines or branches have been immune.

Though weather disruption can happen at almost any time of year (the snow hazard was naturally discussed under winter early in the book), autumn was the time when flooding and storms – the most frequent form of disruption – were commonest. Though hot weather thunderstorms can also cause local havoc, widespread flooding sometimes starts even in mid-summer when a fine spell is broken by what seems the early onset of autumn.

Whatever, the results can be equally disruptive. There are three kinds of flooding: sudden and dramatic flash floods causing washouts including the carrying away of bridges and embankments;

inundations caused by long periods of continuous rain swelling and overflowing rivers; and problems when the sea breaks beyond its usual limits. We call the railway the permanent way, but major structures dating back to Victorian times are rapidly knocked out by once-in-centuries flooding striking different and often very localised areas.

The mere warning of potential trouble causes disruptions. A decade or so ago, when we went to catch the early morning departure of the *Highland Chieftain*, the day's only High Speed Train from Inverness to London, the crew announced that they weren't sure it would be running or not. The driver of the day's only earlier train had reported a jolt as he came to the end of the long curved viaduct near the site of the Culloden Battlefield. Inspection revealed that the embankment might indeed be weakened by water coming off the viaduct. As a precaution, the train was cancelled. We were on our way to an urgent appointment and, just in time to catch the eye of our taxi driver before he left the platform, we asked him to hold on – and eventually take us to Edinburgh. The road following a more direct route, we were able to catch the train from there before our cancelled one.

That, plus one night's cancellation of a train to Aberdeen and of one night's sleeper due to flooding probably typifies the kind of inconvenience suffered in a lifetime of train travel by most of us. Naturally some people are less fortunate; over the years bad weather has cost dozens of lives.

Today there is a well-oiled procedure to arrange bus replacements, but flooding in Victorian times, when the railway had a monopoly, was altogether harder to handle. Few stage coaches survived railway competition, and anyway would have taken a long time to reach the right spot and to travel around the obstructed track, not to mention the fact that they were too small to cope with trainfuls of passengers. This was demonstrated in 1846, just three months after the opening of the North British Railway from Berwick to Edinburgh, when severe flash floods, caused by the heaviest rainfall since the 1770s, severely damaged bridges and culverts over a 19-mile section. It took almost as long to repair the track as it had so far been open.

Though a few lessons are usually learnt, after such exceptional weather generally the best that can be done is to patch and reinstate in the expectation that the next rare weather disaster may be so far into the distance as to be dismissed. However, along the same North British route much greater damage was caused to bridges, culverts and embankments, with sections of track left dangling in mid-air, in 1948. A symbol of post-war recovery, the *Flying Scotsman* was again scheduled to run non-stop to Edinburgh, but on 12 October had to reverse at Alnmouth and return to Newcastle, from where it went via Carlisle to reach the Waverley route – but only to the point where both tracks were blocked by a landslide. So it went back to Carlisle, the third attempt via Carstairs getting it into the Scottish capital ten hours late.

Meanwhile the extent of the damage became clear. It would obviously be many weeks before trains could again run up the East Coast mainline, so priority was given to repairing the branch line via St Boswells and the Waverley route with which it connected. Trains heading for Waverley station off the Waverley route then had to make a zig-zag shunt at the approach to Haymarket. Waverley now being the only main Edinburgh station today, that would not be necessary, but all over Britain relief routes such as were used then have been closed, as have most small mainline stations. That means greater reliance on bus replacements for long journeys, particularly hard on the elderly with heavy luggage who count on being seen off and collected at the beginning and end of the journey. In those days a thousand trucks travelled daily to Edinburgh by the East Coast line, so much of diversionary capacity was taken up by freight. How things have changed with the nearly all-passenger railway running faster and far more frequent trains.

The greatest damage on that occasion was between Berwick and Dunbar: a succession of bridges and culverts were destroyed or damaged while a 52ft-high embankment collapsed. The Royal Engineers used wartime experience to erect temporary bridges. Maybe as many men were at work, among other things removing thousands of tons of debris, and replacing embankments with thousands of cubic feet of soil and stones, as when the line was first built.

Though the effects of the two episodes north of Berwick, flash flood and inundation caused by heavy rain, are the same, inundations are usually gentler affairs, water level rising steadily till tracks and axles are covered and railway stations look more like canal ones, boat movements oddly controlled by signals. I recall (and reported) that happening in Devon in autumn 1960, when repeated heavy rain re-destroyed routes that had been repaired. Several branch lines were closed and the mainline through Exeter St David's repeatedly disrupted, though flooding in towns and on country roads was even worse. Throughout the British Isles there have been times when re-routed trains became blocked by other, newer floods destroying repair work.

Lines of the former Highland and Great North of Scotland Railway have always been specially subject to flood as well as snow troubles. Sooner or later, almost everywhere is affected, some places such as Elgin many times. Usually rail looks to road to help out, but more recently on the edge of the Lake District at Workington, the railway came to the aid when a vital road bridge linking the two parts of the town was washed away. A temporary new North Workington station was built in record time and a shuttle service offered free travel.

Especially when fast-flowing rivers scour the foundations of piers, there are might-have-beens with lucky escapes. On 7 February 1989, a train which had crossed the viaduct over the tidal Ness at Inverness was making its way north when it became one of several trapped on a self-contained system from Muir of Ord to Kyle of Lochalsh, Thurso and Wick. A number of people had earlier reported that there seemed to be erosion of the viaduct piers. It collapsed, leaving the bridge unsupported, the track falling into the river the following day. Replacement took months, a temporary depot being established to maintain the DMUs at Muir of Ord, though passengers were bussed to Dingwall.

Less fortunate were those on the day's first northbound train on the Central Wales line on Monday 19 October 1987. As often in October, the weather had been very wet and anxiety had been

expressed the previous day. Though a Red Alert from the River
Authority had not been passed on to BR, it was thought prudent
to have an operating manager ride on the 05.27 two-car Diesel
from Swansea to Shrewsbury. At a second flood he instructed the
driver to slow down to under 5mph. Where a separate locomotive
wasn't being used, it was permissible for the train itself cautiously
to probe.

When it reached the five-span bridge over the swollen Towy, it
moved very slowly, the staff keenly looking through the light of the
headlamp. It was felt the structure was sound... till – too late to
apply the brake – the driver noticed that a span had collapsed. All
six passengers and three railwaymen went into the river. The rear car
was up-ended but its rear dry. Some people semi-swum and climbed
to safety, but then the front car was turned sideways by the force of
the river and, with a loud crack, three passengers and the driver were
hurled to their death.

As it happens I was with the head of Welsh Railways riding coal
trains down the Valleys that day. He broadcast before we set off and
said there was nothing he could do, though the event clouded our
day and, before the case was dropped, for two years there was the
threat of an action against BR for unlawful killing.

There is hardly a section of coast where rough weather or exceptionally high tides haven't caused damage at some time. The Welsh
Coast has been especially affected. In the 1930s the GWR repaired
erosion along the Cambrian Coast with great determination, but
in more recent time it proved harder to defend vital sections of the
North Wales mainline. It was the same on exposed branch lines

including the Tralee & Dingle in Ireland where, when rough weather was expected, trains were once retimed to avoid high tide.

Everything the sea has done elsewhere fades into insignificance compared to the infamous East Coast floods of 1953. Exceptionally high tides coincided with a gale which uniquely raised the sea level and flooded extensive areas, closing many lines and stations. Though it was serious and caused loss of life and untold hardship, there was a lighter side, as when the paddle steamer providing the ferry across the Humber broke loose, its funnel colliding with and destroying a signal gantry. Gerry Fiennes described it as intervention by providence when the foreman at Harwich carriage sidings was trapped by rising water and saved by a ladder floating by.

There was also amazing endeavour by railwaymen to do their best for passengers and rolling stock. Signalmen have often fared badly. One was cycling home when met by the incoming tide, his cycle found in the road and his body in a garden. That was the only railway fatality, but a signalman at Yarmouth South Town was trapped in his box for twenty one hours till a boat could reach him.

Great was the improvisation as railwaymen fought to restore things to normal, one problem being that many locomotives were marooned. Lifeline freight and commuter services soon struggled back to life, though it was to be several months before everything was repaired... including lines closed a few years later.

Bad weather did however result in the final closure of some lines. A minor but well-known example is the narrow-gauge Corris Railway which, after its slate-carrying and passenger heyday, was struggling with little freight traffic under GWR ownership. It finally closed soon after BR took over – too soon to be rescued by the new volunteer movement now trying to bring part of it back to life. It was a godsend for the Talyllyn, the first line to be reopened by volunteers, where the engines at knock-down prices were very welcome for the unusual gauge the lines shared. Because of their tiny engines, narrow-gauge railways from the Campbeltown & Machrihanish across Scotland's dangling Kintyre peninsula and to Ireland's Tralee & Dingle among others, were especially prone to being brought to a halt by floods.

A major premature closure brought about by heavy rain, though the actual cause was a landslide deeply burying part of the track, was the eastern part of the Callender & Oban. It was already under closure threat and, though there was a bitter local controversy, restoring it wouldn't have been worthwhile. Already a summer tourist train was reaching Oban via the connection with the West Highland at Crianlarich, which has since become the permanent route.

Landslides and avalanches are another risk. Alongside Loch Awe on the section of the C&O which is still open, there has long been semaphore signalling that falling rock is supposed to trigger by hitting the signal wire. However on 6 June 2010 a large rock fell vertically behind the wire and rolled underneath it onto the track derailing the front car of a two-car Diesel set, leaving it sticking up vertically. It was a light summer evening and the driver had time to slow. On a dark winter night he would have hit it at speed: another might have been.

As always, the staff were praised for their efforts to rescue passengers. Removing the vehicle posed a real problem. The parallel road, also closed by the incident, had to be strengthened to allow a large crane to be brought in. Photographs of the vehicle being lifted high before being rerailed appeared in many newspapers and on several television channels.

As we saw in the chapter on snow, there are challenges on all of Scotland's great scenic routes. It perhaps comes as a surprise to say that wind has been responsible for the greatest number of weather-related deaths... until that is one is reminded of the Tay Bridge Disaster, the only British train accident in which everyone on board (a total of seventy five) lost their lives. That the bridge with the train on it was blown down, could have been blamed on shoddy work. As you cross by the slender replacement, the piers of the initial structure are a monument of that terrible night of 18 December 1879.

Though we think of it as an inundation, the infamous East Coast floods and nearly all damage to railways' coastal defences in Britain, Ireland and the world, have actually been caused by the wind The link is clearest seen along the Sea Wall, between Dawlish and Teignmouth, where rough seas driven by strong wind at high tide now routinely causes problems and – with rising water levels – the very existence of Brunel's daring piece of the mainline to the West between cliff and sea is threatened. There is talk of resurrecting a 1930s scheme for an inland route. Many have been the disruptions caused by the sea and cliff falls throughout the line's history. Much money has been spent making the cliffs less perpendicular and netting them, reinstating damage caused by the sea, and reducing the risk of closure. For example, ordinary track circuiting which doesn't work in water has been replaced by sturdier wheel counters, and the up track (slightly further from the waves) is now signalled by bilateral working. More money is invested in making the Cross Country Voyager trains less prone to spray damage. Great Western's HSTs are more resilient.

Damage depends on tide height and direction as well as velocity of the wind, but during my life I've seen conditions steadily worsen as the sea level has risen. Sometimes only ballast is washed away, but the down platform at Dawlish was once largely destroyed, while in furious storms drivers have been known to shelter their train in a tunnel. It is among the best-loved sections of all railways and I have long been thankful to the Teignmouth councillors who had the foresight to agree to Brunel's proposal – providing the railway built and maintained a pedestrian promenade from the exit of the last tunnel at Parson & Clerk into Teignmouth. Don't however be caught walking it when the tide comes in and the seasonal railway is most exposed.

AUTUMN

FOG

IT'S HARD TO become nostalgic about fog, yet for generations train-men, signalmen and fogmen on the lineside (placing detonators on the track) struggled in considerable adversity to keep the wheels turning with their own folklore and traditions. For the most part they suc-ceeded with uncanny safety resulting. Moreover, though conditions were often truly awful, they worked willingly, especially in earlier times when the railways had a virtual monopoly, and there was universal pride in keeping the nation connected.

'Clean air' only came after the common adoption (only the pio-neering GWR already had a version) of 'automatic train control', and most serious fogs and smogs were before the days of extensive track circuiting and electric light signals with piercing beams. Today's railway would seem a doddle to those who relied on far less sophisticated infrastructure when it was sometimes hard to see clearly across a station leave alone the length of a few coaches. Difficulties began with fog signallers having to be called out by a messenger. Few if any were on the telephone.

Late autumn including the run up to Christmas, was the traditional time for fog to which the railways themselves contributed not a little. Even in my time, I recall many a crisp sunny morning in the village of Ipplepen where I lived, but having to crawl only five miles away to reach Newton Abbot station with its dozens of locomotives steaming and smoking away being prepared for their working day or at the end of it, along with a dirty coal-driven power station.

There are still extensive rules for handling the traffic in fog and falling snow both in the rule book and working timetable, but there is much less need to consult them today. In the past, on some routes trains were kept two blocks apart but, whether or not that was the case, peak-time services were thinned down, especially in suburban areas. Even so, in the worst fogs, especially in the days before the First World War when signalling was often more primitive, there were horrendous hold ups, seriously delaying passengers, Christmas mail and freight of all kinds. For example, on 20 December 1891, a fog descended on the London area that persisted until the evening of Christmas Day. At times fog signalmen were unable to tell the aspect of the signal they were standing under, or even to see each other yards apart. With fog also in the industrial north, up trains were seriously late reaching London.

Delay breeds delay. Trains had to make extra stops to cover cancelled or connecting services.

In the days before extensive water troughs, or in fog accompanied by frost, there was often an extra delay for taking on water. Even if the water troughs were not actually frozen, it was feared that splashes might freeze, disabling the brakes. A station stop involved manually signalling 'right of way' from the guard at the back to the driver. In pea soupers that meant it being repeated by a battery of porters close enough to pass it on.

At termini, late arrivals could mean late departures and, at any major centre, staff might had problems finding their way round carriage sidings and locomotive sheds. Especially in horse-drawn days, passengers and mail were naturally also seriously delayed by fog on city streets.

In pea soupers, goods trains had sometimes to be abandoned, left in sidings or loops till conditions cleared, in the worst cases, as again in 1904, for days until the fog lifted.

Livestock on the way to Smithfield Show or to be butchered in big cities caused especial problems. Cattle need watering, and eventually their trucks cleaned. At least once, such were the delays that the stock had to be destroyed in transit… nasty in itself and leaving a trail of confusion, losses and claims.

There were still pea soupers even after the Second World War, but by then road transport had taken over much freight, and the burden was shared. I have several fog memories of my own, such as rushing to catch a train about to depart from Rochdale and collapsing on the wooden stairway up to the platform having taken in so much impurity that my lungs temporarily gave out. In Newcastle-upon-Tyne, a basket of apples was rendered uneatable until rewashed because particles of dirt suspended in the air had formed a black crust on their sticky surface.

One recalls that once smarter businessmen put on a fresh collar for the afternoon.

When, in the mid-1930s, the family lived in Gidea Park, I recall Dad returning late from Town with stories of how, on his morning journey, one moment he had been in bright sunshine, the next almost blind, the train crawling and stopping, trusting the railwaymen to prevent another train running into his. In fog, and even when conditions threatened it, many regulars ensured they travelled toward the front away from any rear-end collision, though the middle might have been safer. The irony was always that if it were not for the fog, it would be a clear sunny day.

Some of the accidents in fog were down to its transience, fog working not being imposed soon enough when things were suddenly blotted out and fog signalmen struggled to reach their posts, occasionally not even being able to tell which tracks were the mainline. That is what happened at a notorious crash at Gidea Park, just up the road from where we had lived – on 2 January 1947, at the beginning of the LNER's extremely difficult last year.

Among the seven passengers killed (another forty five were injured) I was told there was one who had always insisted on travelling toward the front, but on this occasion was delayed by the fog in London for his return journey from Liverpool Street and jumped into the crowded rear just before it started. A following express crashed into it.

For the technically minded, the official accident report makes interesting reading. As often is the case, there were a number of contributing factors. Gidea Park was between semaphore signalling on the London side and modern electric signalling to the east, installed in 1934 when the local lines were extended to Shenfield. The signalling between Romford and Gidea Park was transitional semaphores, partly worked automatically with miniature lower repeater arms. But for the war, electric light automatic signalling would long have been introduced throughout.

The driver of the train crashed into, the 10.28pm from Liverpool Street to Southend-on-Sea, said he had difficulty in reading some, but significantly not all, the signals approaching Romford and in the cutting through to Gidea Park. His guard had just given the all clear and grasped the rail on his van about to get on board as the train started moving, but saved his life when he didn't do so – as the locomotive of the delayed 10.25pm express to Peterborough charged into it at full speed. Several carriages were demolished and others derailed.

Fog was frequent, yet Romford signalbox lacked a lever to place an emergency detonator on the track, something found even at many boxes on GWR single-line branches. The signalman said that might have saved the day when he realised the Peterborough express had not slowed down after passing Gidea Park's distant signal at caution. The delay in the fog signalmen not reaching their post (and their inconsistent evidence) was crucial, while the Gidea Park signalman also shared part of the blame for allowing his outer home to show clear before he was sure the express had reduced speed.

Both signalmen were left helpless, waiting for the accident to happen. Most blamed was the driver of the Peterborough express for maintaining high speed when reading the miniature repeater semaphores had been difficult, fog being thicker here than in the London area... and, after catching a glimpse of one on his trackside way, that he should have assumed that fog signallers were not all at their posts. In fact a member of staff on Gidea Park's other island platform said that, going at that speed, the driver of the approaching express must have been 'driving on his bangs'. In fog, two detonators were placed on the line about six feet apart ahead of the distance signal if it showed caution and thus the home signal could be at danger. The lack of bangs implied all clear. A fog signalman showed a flag of appropriate colour. It was also questioned whether the Gidea Park signalman had used the switch to fog working, lengthening track-circuit control.

Especially when they have happened in fog, accidents seem almost to have been inevitable. There must have actually been many potential accidents that didn't happen, allowing staff who had slipped up to breathe again. Yet overall the wonder is that without automatic train control, safety was generally assured. In this case the Peterborough express had only been four minutes behind from the Southend train all the way to Romford, where only the Southend stopped. The Southend train had however lost seventeen minutes because of the conditions, and no doubt some of its passengers were apprehensive – but then again most apprehension was and is quite unnecessary… certainly compared to driving on a road in fog.

After England's worst-ever railway accident on 8 October 1952, it took the outrage of public opinion to force the nationwide introduction of automatic train control. A late-running Perth-Euston sleeping car express crashed into a local at Harrow & Wealdstone on London's outskirts. Significantly, on that occasion fog signalling had just been abandoned, but a pocket of fog probably contributed to the Perth train's driver over-running signals. Such was the volume of suburban traffic, that the signalman had correctly switched the local from slow to fast lines for the rest of the trip into Euston, and signals were properly set. Here the oft quoted 'might have beens' actually happened, the strewn wreckage rapidly run into a minute later by a double-headed down express.

'Automatic train control' is better described as an automatic warning, a bell ringing in the cab if the next signal is green, but a siren warning if it is yellow or red. While the brake is applied if the driver doesn't respond, it is easy for him to acknowledge it but fail to reduce speed. The danger on congested lines, especially in rush hour, is that drivers, not passing a signal at green or hearing the all-clear bell for many miles, can become too routine or automatic in their acknowledgement and cancellation of the warning. Against that, in today's much rarer and less serious fogs, drivers especially appreciate the warning, possibly making it even safer to be travelling in fog than at other times.

A final backward glance, to December 1952, as it happens only weeks after the Harrow & Wealdstone accident. Now it wasn't the transitional nature of fog, but a long-lasting greeny-yellow pea souper that brought London to a standstill and was so bad that it, like the accident, finally awoke the public conscience. For days it was impossible to get round the capital in a normal manner. Bus services were abandoned, and so many resorted to the Underground that there were reports of picnicking among crowds waiting for a train they could force themselves onto.

On Friday 5 December, a journey from Aldershot to Waterloo which should have taken about forty five minutes lasted hours, with constant stopping and starting. Only slowly it dawned on passengers that there was a smog. They didn't realised when the train finally reached Waterloo. 'The guard came along hammering on the doors, "Get out, get out". You couldn't see the platform. You had to take it on trust.'

Two days later the stock finally arrived for the Smithfield Show. Many fine animals were seriously distressed: ten had to be put down, and several more died. The fog cut visibility in the building, as it did in some theatres where performances had to be cancelled. Harold Macmillan, then the Housing Minister whose performance was ultimately widely respected, wasn't sure that preventing smog was a government responsibility. The public now felt otherwise. Indeed it actually spelt the end of days of laissez-faire.

They were not happy times, for less than two months later 133 people met their death in a storm on the railway ferry *Princess Victoria* on her way from Stranraer to Larne. As in accidents involving fog, the enquiry revealed considerable negligence.

Today it is on our motorways that fog is dreaded with, it seems, occasionally inevitable multi-crashes. No wonder many who usually travel by road resort to trains in difficult conditions.

And at such times it is marvellous seeing crowds alight from punctual trains. But give a thought to the unsung heroes of past pea soupers, including those in shunting yards.

TRAINS THROUGH THE NIGHT

FOR MUCH OF railway history, people disliked making an early start but were happy travelling overnight. Not merely were there sleepers, whole trains and single or pairs of cars, to many places (even between Inverness, Edinburgh and Glasgow), but every night thousands sat in compartments of trains travelling more slowly and having longer station stops than by day. I used to know some people, including relatives, oddballs perhaps, who felt that a night spent even on a crowded train saved a day. In a curious way, too, they found it companionable being on the move when others were asleep in their beds.

Much the same could be said for that rare breed, sleeping car attendants. They undoubtedly felt they were someone just because of their lonely and unusual work, putting their passengers to bed and remaining on call. Their traffic and travelling conditions were much affected by the season.

The same applied even more strongly to those who staffed the Travelling Post Offices. Here the companionship came from a close-knit team of like-minded skilful colleagues working together night after night.

Indeed, many enginemen, guards and signalmen, even platform staff, commented that, though adjusting to shift changes could be hard, night work brought its own satisfaction. Many were the tales I heard of nocturnal working practices and the greater feeling of purpose brought by working in the wee hours. There was a great, yet generally unhurried sense of responsibility – and also a close seasonal affinity, and interest in night wildlife.

Much less happens now by night, large parts of the network being idle. But once the West Coast mainline was actually busier by night than day. There were sleeper, passenger and Motorail trains, postal, newspaper, perishable and parcel and all manner of goods ones.

When I was a boy at Teignmouth, on a still night the distant sound of metal wheels on rails alongside the Teign Estuary seldom died away for long – and was continuous at the peak of the West Cornwall broccoli season when numerous specials had to be slotted in. Not that the Great Western was ever as busy at night as the West Coast mainline. 'There's a train in the section just as much of the time as in the day, but the sections are longer [intermediate boxes switched out] and they travel more slowly,' a signalman once told me.

When I moved to Ipplepen, near Dainton summit, if sleep was elusive, the sound of a train engine responding to the banker's whistles could soon be heard, followed by the music of the two machines struggling up to Dainton tunnel, usually steadily but occasionally with much slipping and adjustment of the regulator.

But then, wherever one went, at home or abroad, trains were a feature of the night time as much as the owls' screeched greetings to one another. At times it was trains on the move, fast or slow; at others of endless shunting, with the clang of buffers in the days that loose-coupled trucks were fly-shunted down different tracks. The hotel at Launceston in Tasmania was uncomfortably close to the goods yard, where goods trains seemed to arrive and be broken up and remade all night, albeit the sole remaining daily passenger train, connecting with those in either direction on the mainline, had been withdrawn shortly before my visit.

It was as passengers were prepared to make an earlier start, and the first expresses especially to London, arrived progressively earlier, that patronage of the sleepers began its remorseless decline, and people like a cousin of mine also began complaining that it was harder to make a journey by night in an ordinary carriage. Better roads and internal flights also took their toll, though British Rail, always prone to exaggerated fears of the moment, didn't help by driving passengers away. After a couple of cases of nocturnal alcohol abuse, sitting passengers were barred from sleeper trains. When protests were made, it was decided they might travel in a sub-contracted carriage. Burdensome red tape soon put a stop to that.

Now sitting passengers are happily carried on all sleepers. All? It is down to a mere three a night to London, two from Scotland, though separate sections serve five starting points, and one from Cornwall. Regular users fear that when the present stock is life-expired, it will be the end of the sleeping car as it has been for the Travelling Post Office, Motorail, cattle, milk and so many other night trains.

If you are prepared to make an early start and return later, day train trips to London are possible from all Britain including just beyond Scotland's Central Belt – though certainly not from Inverness.

Much the same thing has happened in Ireland where overnight services have ceased but many trains to Dublin start at what was once an unheard of hour, except for the few actually working through the night. The trend is similar across Europe and indeed most of the world, though decisively not in India where the railways still reflect surprisingly British influences of yesteryear and all human life is enacted on long journeys including night travel.

In Britain if one talks of going by sleeper today, friends think it odd (or romantic) and are surprised to hear and only half believe that it is actually comfortable and soothing. The irony is that, while people are reluctant to travel by rail overnight, record numbers do so in far less comfort on planes. Is it simply because air travel is more up-to-date? One could site the analogy of bosses never touching a typewriter because that was secretaries' work but happily keying their own memos on computers.

It would be wrong to give the impression that, if life were generally slower at night, staff didn't have to work attentively. In many working timetables, the Travelling Post Offices carried a note saying that everyone concerned with their operation should note that punctuality was imperative.

Even if a milk or other perishable train ran late, it could seriously upset the distribution system. But in the run up to Christmas, sleepers that also handled mail and parcel traffic, could be notoriously late. Long gone are the days of those trains (I still have one on my model railway) that carried mail, parcels, sleeping and sitting cars and perhaps a rudimentary buffet. They epitomised the bits-and-pieces nature of night business on many secondary routes.

In the week before Christmas, mail was so heavy that it would have overwhelmed the Travelling Post Offices and so the sorters were deployed at depots. At other times they were supreme, because a tight-knit system united England, Wales and Scotland, making it possible for a letter posted over a large part of the country to be delivered early next morning, a level of service not quite maintained today. Letters could be posted in a special late box on the trains themselves or, at many places, a late box beside the ordinary letter box just outside the station.

So in Newton Abbot a letter to anywhere in the country could be posted up to ten o'clock at night, hours after the last ordinary collection had been cleared. Collected by someone off the TPO, if it were for, say, Plymouth, it would travel to Bristol, where the up and down Great Western TPOs (so called till the end) exchanged mail between themselves as well as those from South Wales and the north. Beyond Truro, Penzance's mail – all of it – was sorted into street delivery order and, on arrival, handed to the postmen so they could immediately set off on their rounds. It was a luxurious but expensive system.

It seemed too good to be true when a new fleet of vehicles was built for an extended TPO network along with a few special stations within new Royal Mail depots, and so it soon proved. The total transfer to air and road was soon announced, and all the new stock laid up, though some is again in use for a regular service to Scotland and for peak times and emergencies, as when air travel was halted because of Icelandic volcanic ash in early 2010. Those manning the TPOs were the elite of postal staff, sorting letters with amazing dexterity, and having marvellous knowledge, taking especial pride in sorting out where to send badly or incompletely-addressed letters. Few stayed on with Royal Mail when their specialist work ceased.

I saw them at work twice, once when mail was still exchanged at speed, the arm extended out from the train after the appropriate bridge or landmark had been passed... whatever the weather. 'Stand clear' could be heard just before the incoming bags arrived with great force, instantly to be collected by the appropriate sorter. How everything was accomplished at speed without the least hint of panic was wonderful to behold.

Just how important timing was and what decisions had to be taken was made evident at Bristol Temple Meads on the down run one night, when I was recording a broadcast. The train with the York TPO had been delayed. Dozens of men from the Bristol sorting office had taken away many truckloads of mail and loaded many more, the exchanges had been made between ourselves and the up TPO and the South Wales one, and departure time was on us. If we 'saved the mail' we'd leave a good five minutes late.

'It's borderline,' the inspector said to me. 'You decide.'

What responsibility. I opted to wait, and many people received letters from the north by first instead of second delivery. We made up time, but meanwhile held up a goods train that was to follow us... and, delay breeding delay, that could have reacted on later services.

Much the same wasteful thing happened as the older sleeping cars (with often-quoted notice that no solid matter should be put in the potty in the compartment to be tipped out onto the line through an internal connection) were replaced by modern ones, the mark IIIs still in use.

These were well on the way to being built when, on 6 July 1978, fire broke out in one of the pair of Plymouth sleepers added to the Penzance-Paddington service. Linen stacked against a radiator caught fire. Twelve people died, mainly from fumes, after failing to find a door that would open. To protect their passengers from potential interruption, but against the rules, most attendants kept the cars locked. There was naturally an outcry, and the completion of the new vehicles was seriously delayed for the incorporation of new safety features.

This happened just at the time that earlier and faster morning business services to London were being introduced, and the bad publicity resulting from the accident also hurt demand. Many of the new sleepers were never used though, while it was still possible under single management, British Rail ran a long hotel train with varied itineraries, some nights spent on board, others in a hotel. I regularly saw the long, even rake plus restaurant car pass under the window of the room at which I worked at David & Charles, an alternative early morning point of interest being the occasional passage of the Royal Train, parked on a branch line overnight.

The majority of the sleepers were ultimately broken up, the Scottish services now having few spares. Then, in vain, we looked forward to the day we could go to bed in Edinburgh or Bristol and wake up in Paris. After the rolling stock had been built and well tested, it was decreed there was inadequate demand. The sleepers built to international standards were mothballed and eventually sold to Via, the Canadian passenger train operator. Though most passengers were disturbed by the excruciating squeaks and bumps of being shunted on and off the ferry, once you could go to bed in London and wake up in Paris. It was the kind of one-off service that – decades before the Channel Tunnel – BR killed off as soon as public opinion allowed.

So, our sleepers survive on borrowed time, but it is remarkable that new crews (now of women as well as men) are readily found willing and indeed enthusiastic about their peculiar nocturnal lifestyle. Many are the colourful individuals I have been put to bed by over the years, including on Motorail trains and regular routes such as Manchester-Plymouth and Euston to Corkickle (just outside Whitehaven) once popular with those working at Sellafield's nuclear plant, that have long been a fading memory.

CHRISTMAS

CHRISTMAS AND THE railways served each other well; of that there is no doubt. What was to have been my second sentence is more suspect. 'The railway inherited and greatly expanded the colourful seasonal business and traditions till then chiefly associated with the stage coach.' On reflection, the truth is that Christmas had been in the doldrums since Cromwell and the Commonwealth. The spirit of Christmas as we know it was almost a joint invention of Dickens and the railways. It was fortuitous that publication of the *Pickwick Papers* (1837) with Mr Pickwick and company travelling on the Muggleton coach ('well wrapt up in great-coats, shawls and comforters') to spend Christmas with old Wardle and the fat boy at Dingley Dell, virtually coincided with the opening of the first trunk line, the London & Birmingham (1838).

That the stage coach is a popular theme for today's cards is more because of the glow of nostalgia than that they were really appreciated in their era. What history more accurately records are complains about the oppressive atmosphere and smells inside, shivering on uncomfortable seating outside, and no space being available for journeys needing to be taken in a hurry, together with over-charging and poor service at inns en route.

The one thing that stage coaches proved was the value of speed, schedules being steadily shortened, timings down to half minutes, during their brief heyday. To that extent the railway did indeed rapidly build on established foundations. When new railways opened, the declining stage coach was instantly relegated to acting as their feeder services. The railways spread and rapidly became more sophisticated, and Dickens increasingly capitalised on the Christmas spirit. Both had a profound effect. *A Christmas Carol* was published in 1843. Dickens was a powerful influence, especially in the drawing rooms of the influential. Like today's mail-order companies, and one might say almost foreseeing the internet, Dickens worked hard to be close to his audience. His monthly *Household Words* begun in 1850 had for those days a huge readership, enjoying a new Christmas story each December.

The spread of the railway and their usage were both phenomenal. To cite one example: by the end of the century, Christmas Eve saw well over a thousand trains depart from Waterloo, nearly all long-distance ones having at least one relief section. Though, as we will see in a moment, goods and parcels traffics were more lucrative, inevitably one starts with the glamour of the passenger side.

That included school trains, many disgorging their happy cargoes at Paddington around the same time, a few days before Christmas, and the start of people going away for a break at an hotel as well as staying with friends. Until relatively recent times, an important feature was the journey home for the growing number of those pursuing careers in London and other cities. It was indeed a vital part of the celebration, with greater expectation than enjoyed today when Britain plc closes down for a long period.

Christmas was far more than just time off work. Its spirit was especially strong on late evening trains on Christmas Eve and on the 'get-you-home' services on Christmas morning for those whose work didn't finish early enough to travel on Christmas Eve. In the days when trunk telephone calls were a luxury, and those for Christmas Day had to be booked ahead, and were rationed to three minutes before the first pips pipped, just being able to hug parents or children brought relief, joy and tears. In many families with relatives who had emigrated and in pre-jet days couldn't afford the time to return home by ship, extra emotion was released just being back with those who stayed in Britain. I'll return to this theme at the chapter's end.

Nowhere was the sense of Christmas travel excitement greater than at Euston. The taxi sweeping between the Doric columns of the pair of 72ft high porticos made many tingle. This was perhaps the greatest symbol of the Railway Age, the London & Birmingham Railway directors spending what was then the princely sum of £35,000 on it to celebrate the pride of their achievement. Again that was in 1838, the year before the first railway hotels – a pair of them also at Euston – opened, pioneering railway hotels beside many important stations in London and the provinces.

Today's Euston may be more functional, but is unloved. Carols, traditionally led by the vicar of St Pancras, were sung in the old Great Hall, a superb room though scarcely convenient for passengers in a hurry. When eventually the right platform was found, the train was usually ready for boarding, twenty unhurried minutes before departure. If you believed in travelling in style, the thing to do was to collect your meal ticket from the steward on the platform beside the restaurant car – or cars, with a kitchen car sandwiched between the first and third-class coaches. The sumptuous LMS 12-wheeled restaurant cars were the world's best, and ventured out even on 25th December. A famous LMS photograph showed the chef displaying his offerings on the platform on Christmas morning.

Working on Christmas Day brought its own pleasures, with little feeling of resentment. Indeed extra staff were sometimes required to meet the needs of those attracted by the special cheap excursion tickets on Christmas Day and Boxing Day, when thousands went to their nearest theatre for the first day of the pantomime. To cite another example, the Great Northern alone carried 500 actors from London to appear in Christmas pantomimes.

Only gradually, and well into nationalised days, was the Christmas Day train service seriously trimmed back and then abandoned. In Scotland, a full morning commuter service ran, in the same way that, in all but its northerly extremities, England went to work on New Year's Day. Again, well into BR days, Boxing Day was also once busy, until – in the 1950s – services were thinned down almost to Sunday levels, though several trains ran on some branch lines that were normally closed on Sundays.

As a young journalist working away from home, I regularly travelled on Boxing Day morning, either to get back to work or to go home for a delayed Christmas lunch. For journalists, the Christmas break was either Christmas Day or Boxing Day, never both. In a sense the circle has been completed, for now the total shut-down for at least two days is used for major engineering works employing many staff at premium rates.

Until the 1930s, everything needed for Christmas came by railway including (by post or the railways own parcels business) all the presents from distant relatives and friends. To cite a further example thanks to Charles H Grinling's *The Ways of Our Railways* published in several editions in the first years of the 20th century, in the week before Christmas the LNWR alone carried 35,000 Christmas hampers north out of London. Hamper companies were one of many Christmas businesses made possible by the railways.

Even in the 1950s, the railway was predominant. Most letters posted on Christmas Eve were delivered on Christmas morning, when postmen still met trains at many stations and sorted the mail before the last seasonal rounds set off.

Parcel clerks made a real effort to ensure the railway's own last parcels were delivered… or at least phoned their recipients to say they were ready for collection. All part of the job gladly done.

Traditionally, the big rush of goods traffic has always been well before Christmas. As shops stocked up, and as the holiday approached, staff and trucks were re-allocated to swell the ranks of the hard-pressed parcels side. Livestock for Smithfield was a vital business, followed by a rush of dead stock, including increasingly important meat from the Commonwealth, in the last week, when more perishables including poultry, fish and milk were carried. The railway particularly encouraged the eating of best Scottish beef in Southern England, priority given to the parcels expresses carrying it south. At one time, 4,000 wagons of livestock passed through Aberdeen in the week before Christmas.

Considering how short the Christmas holiday was in those days, the quantity of food consumed was prodigious. When general diets were more spartan, the Christmas dinner stood out as a great luxurious multi-course leisurely occasion when far more would be eaten than today. There was always turkey or other meat left over for sandwiches for dear ones leaving all too soon to start their return journey. Such was the importance of the parcels business that even when Christmas Day passenger services were abandoned, perishable traffic, including milk, was still carried. A pair of both parcel and milk trains ran up the main line from Plymouth, for example.

My own memories of Christmas on the railways are inevitably of the West Country. Strongest of all is of several Christmas Eve trips just after the war made to South Molton, where we had been evacuated for a couple of years and I still knew many people including the signalmen. Trains were busy, the surprise being the number using the last up service of the day.

Food was still scarce in most of Britain, but not in South Molton. I recall being one of five men who got into a non-corridor compartment. Almost furtively we put our parcels and bags onto the rack or tucked them tightly beside us on the floor. The compartment was veritably stuffed with poultry, eggs, and all manner of foods that our womenfolk would undoubtedly welcome. Later, led by a red-faced gent, who had taken a few swigs from his hip flask, we relaxed sufficiently to reveal what each of us had. The line was that, even if it were technically rationed, it might otherwise have gone to waste, for in the land of milk and honey most farming families registered with a grocer but were generally self-sufficient. Tea was the one scarce thing they occasionally went to town to collect.

Chocolate? Little was yet consumed in the relatively primitive countryside and my off-the-ration bar was my personal property, safely guarded as trains were changed at Dulverton and Exeter St David's. Only joining the day's last and crowded express from Paddington to Plymouth did I feel slightly embarrassed carrying much of the family's Christmas fare. As it happened, twice I stood in the corridor next to a former classmate now working in London and returning home for Christmas: my trouser pocket burst, emptying coins onto the floor on one occasion; his on the other.

The build up to Christmas was less commercial then and often the railways provided many special touches such as paper chains in the restaurant cars of certain stewards (in those days they stayed with their own) as well as essential services running the

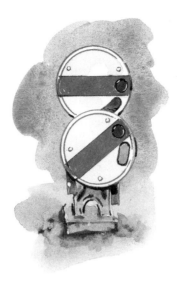

length and breadth of the pre-Beeching system. As already mentioned, a combination of bad weather, heavy mail traffic (though
special mail trains relieved the pressure on key expresses) and – in
the final build up to the holiday – many trains running in several
parts, left punctuality much to be desired. Passengers do weigh,
putting extra strain on the engine, and large numbers take longer
getting on and off. A familiar part of the Christmas ritual was
the crowds waiting for the delayed arrival of their loved ones.
Until the delayed train was finally drawing near, many kept warm
enjoying a drink in the station buffet or a local pub. It was not the
time of year to economise. But all would be on the platform eager
to spot those they were meeting.

Now back to people who had emigrated. There were hundreds
of thousands of them. The three-minute Christmas Day call cost

a fortune. The Royal broadcast was listened to eagerly throughout the Commonwealth uniting folk in a way that has long eroded. News from countries such as Australia and New Zealand meant more, too. Never before or since had Britons felt so much empathy for New Zealand than on Christmas Day 1953, when few travelled across the oceans. We woke up to hear of a terrible accident – the worst, it turned out, in the history of New Zealand railways. Loaded with holidaymakers, much of the Wellington-Auckland express had crashed into an angry river. 161 people were killed, carriages and the concrete piers of the bridge demolished by a flash flood were swept half a mile down stream.

Normally the water was ankle deep, but a natural ice plug had melted, releasing a lake-full of water that gushed down as the train approached. A lone motorist hearing the roar desperately signalled to the train driver who applied the emergency brake seconds before losing his life. We were all stunned and for the first (and except for those who now fly there for a holiday) last time, learned about New Zealand topography. Even when Mum served our turkey, I couldn't get the accident out of my mind.

coupled with a determination that the burial should be a decent one. Old photographs and newspaper cuttings were shown around, wreaths displayed on locomotive fronts, cameras flashed. 'Auld Lang Syne' was sung, someone usually played an instrument even when there was no band. Free use was made of the locomotive whistle, and steam let off as the fireman had made an unnecessarily generous blaze. Cheers went up as the final train started, and exploding detonators, more usually used as fog signals, echoed up the valley.

On such occasions, I often met an elderly passenger or two who had also travelled by the first train, for on some lines passenger trains ran for less than eighty or so years. At the other extreme were children, teenagers and even young adults making their first as well as last journey on the line, sometimes their first railway journey anywhere. Mourners included local bigwigs, perhaps drinking champagne in a reserved compartment, and an itinerant band of enthusiasts who attended all such funerals in their area, occasionally celebrating or mourning the closure of more than one line on the same evening.

On branch lines where the day's last train was normally stabled at the terminus, the stock was usually returned as a special working to a main-line depot. Though not all intermediate stations might be served, usually officials allowed passengers to travel. I've vivid memories of the last advertised train to Princetown on a windy Dartmoor. We alighted on the unusually busy platform while the two engines needed for the extra load of six coaches and a van ran round and then backed what had become the rear into the goods shed where milk for the trainless Monday morning was unloaded. The train then returned to the platform to pick us up, only stopping at Dousland before reversing again at Yelverton. We wondered how milk would reach Princetown in future and how prison warders and their families who made up much of the traffic would fare on the skeleton replacement bus service. Soon they all bought cars.

But there were exceptions where the public were denied access to return workings. 'It's advertised as empty stock, and if you travel by it it won't be,' said by a harassed guard made a super headline for my report of the Helston line's closure for the regional morning paper. The poor guard was mercilessly teased about it by colleagues, though more real embarrassment should have been felt by the district manager. Though I had found out it would, he had three times denied the stock would leave the terminus. 'Do you think you know more about the system than I do?' would honestly have been answered in the affirmative, so disorganised had BR's management become as traffic bled away, losses mounted and morale dipped in the pre-Beeching days.

Since buses were generally cheaper, more frequent and went right into town centres and villages, after the First World War increasingly country trains lingered on with declining and specialist passenger patronage. One group were people starting out on longer journeys, to London or an important regional centre. Though only a handful might connect at the junction on any one occasion, they were journeys of supreme importance and over a period involved many people. A few made journeys to or from villages with no bus. Then there were railwaymen with privilege tickets, mothers with prams that couldn't be taken onto a bus... and in later times increasingly railway enthusiasts.

I recall a train to Lossiemouth with just six passengers... all enthusiasts. Though it would have resulted in earlier closures which wouldn't have pleased us, little hardship would have been caused had trains been replaced by well-timed and reliable bus services on something like forty per cent of country routes from the early 1930s. Before the war, only the LNER seriously experimented with closing stations to passengers while keeping them open for parcels as well as freight, separate parcel trains being run. Even then the buses didn't run to the mainline station, for under the 1930 Road Transport Act (an evil thing) railways were forced to sell their then substantial bus services but were allowed to remain shareholders in bus companies. That allowed neither competition nor co-operation.

Since imported oil was scarcer than home-produced coal, war in 1939 temporarily put the clock back. Ironically, some lines were at their busiest passenger-wise within years of closure. While

there is no doubt that the Beeching cuts went too far – and it is interesting to note that where lines have reopened the deliberately pessimistic estimates of the 'experts' have been systematically well beaten – what utterly failed were the subsidised replacement buses. Given the specialist nature of most remaining business, and the utter lack of sensible co-operation, that is not surprising. Even where initially bus connections were made with mainline trains, they quickly fell out of sync. So as television reporter I pointed to empty buses arriving well after the trains they were supposed to connect with had left, in one case running down a long drive to the junction station well after it had also been closed. Sadly, an integrated transport system, even in areas of sparse population where competition between services is especially ridiculous, is as elusive as ever today.

Closures were not confined to branch lines. Whole systems such as the Somerset & Dorset which on summer Saturdays saw queues of trains panting up onto the Mendips on their way out of Bath, and the equally colourful Midland & Great Northern carrying Midland holidaymakers to Norfolk – both really glorified largely single-track branches but with their own branch lines too – were closed in an uproar of opposition. Scotland lost several double-track mainlines, including the Waverley route from Edinburgh to Carlisle; part of it is being expensively rebuilt mainly for commuters at the Edinburgh end. In all these cases, as with the Settle & Carlisle which BR also wished to get rid of but is busier than ever today, things were deliberately, cynically run-down to help support the closure case.

Many lines are genuinely missed, some for purely nostalgic or for highly uneconomic reasons such as that trains provided a useful fall back when snow and ice made roads unusable, others because they still offered useful year-round service.

Railway nostalgia is big business, most lines being the subject of at least one album and included in a commercial video or DVD. Artists make livings recreating the railway's past. There are literally hundreds of Station Roads with no station, while Hallwill Junction is one of several villages still named after its initial raison d'être. Station houses are now sought after rural residences.

Though steadily eroding through development and reclaimed by farmers, embankments and cuttings, including those of temporary lines serving the building of remote reservoirs can be seen all over the country. Tunnels have been put to many uses, and fine viaducts preserved, such as by the Northern Viaduct Trust. Cycleways follow many old routes, happily sharing formations with restored voluntary steam railways. And there are thousands of miles of the most telling of all clues: bands of woodland that have taken over the railway land.

Incidentally, there has been much confusion about closing dates. I recall receiving carbon copies of a succession of letters exchanged between a pair of authors particular about detail. One said that lines were closed on the day the last train ran; the other that they were closed as and from the first trainless day when services normally ran. On routes with no Sunday service that meant the Monday, the day but one after, the last train. Though the first author exploded that Sunday did exist with people being born and dying on it, BR formally adopted 'as from', the first day that the service didn't run.

Freight continued on many lines after they lost their passenger service. Because the engineering department insisted on a high level of track maintenance, the cost of carriage per ton per mile was ridiculously uneconomic. Indeed, occasional special passenger trains could still run at their old speed. I enjoyed travelling along the old lines by many enthusiasts' specials, but have particularly vivid memories of taking what happened to be the very last train to Bellingham in Northumberland. That was from Morpeth. Though a Diesel, we ran in steam timings, reaching everywhere early, and at some stations had time to stretch our legs and see passengers still arriving in good time to buy the last-ever tickets sold through the booking window hatch. Though only for a single shift, stations still retained staff. We reversed at Redesmouth onto the Border Counties line and were piped into Bellingham en fete for its autumn show. The time is coming when many lines will have been closed for as long as they were open. Though few may realise just what social and economic impact they wrought, they'll never be forgotten.

ACKNOWLEDGEMENTS

ILLUSTRATIONS ARE BY David Charlesworth, who it has been a pleasure to work with. Adrian Sanderson turned my messy manuscript into the final copy that appears in these pages.

As always, my wife Sheila advised as the non-specialist reader and is fun to work with. And the role of my daughter-in-law Benny in suggesting this book has already been mentioned in the first chapter.

This is the third of my books to be published by Frances Lincoln, whose proprietor John Nicholl (he recently introduced us to St Pancras Grand restaurant on the station platform to discuss the title) and staff have been very supportive.

The fourth coming out at the same time is a new edition of my classic *The Country Railway* of 1976 (170,000 copies in print).

The fifth book to appear in their list will be another railway one, a grand *Farewell to Trains,* quite different from any railway book yet seen. Above all thanks to my many appreciative readers who make continuing my writing into my eighties more enjoyable than putting my feet up,